EUCHARIST

Stephen J. Binz

TWENTY THIRD 23rd
PUBLICATIONS
www.23rdpublications.com

Fifth printing 2014

TWENTY-THIRD PUBLICATIONS
A Division of Bayard
One Montauk Avenue, Suite 200
New London, CT 06320
(860) 437-3012 or (800) 321-0411
www.23rdpublications.com

ISBN 978-1-58595-357-8

Library of Congress Catalog Card Number: 2004117873
Printed in the U.S.A.

Contents

LESSONS 13–18

LESSONS 19–24

LESSONS 25–30

How to Use
Threshold Bible Study

Each book in the Threshold Bible Study series is designed to lead you through a new doorway of biblical awareness, to accompany you across a unique threshold of understanding. The characters, places, and images that you encounter in each of these topical studies will help you explore fresh dimensions of your faith and discover richer insights for your spiritual life.

Threshold Bible Study covers biblical themes in depth in a short amount of time. Unlike more traditional Bible studies that treat a biblical book or series of books, Threshold Bible Study aims to address specific topics within the entire Bible. The goal is not for you to comprehend everything about each passage, but rather for you to understand what a variety of passages from different books of the Bible reveals about the topic of each study.

Threshold Bible Study offers you an opportunity to explore the entire Bible from the viewpoint of a variety of different themes. The commentary that follows each biblical passage launches your reflection about that passage and helps you begin to see its significance within the context of your contemporary experience. The questions following the commentary challenge you to understand the passage more fully and apply it to your own life. The prayer starter helps conclude your study by integrating learning into your relationship with God.

These studies are designed for maximum flexibility. Each study is presented in a workbook format, with sections for reading, reflecting, writing, discussing, and praying. Space for writing after each question is ideal for personal study and allows group members to prepare in advance for their discussion. The thirty lessons in each topic may be used by an individual over the period of a month, or by a group for six sessions, with lessons to be studied each week before the next group meeting. These studies are ideal for Bible study groups, small Christian communities, adult faith formation, student groups, Sunday school, neighborhood groups, and family reading, as well as for individual learning.

The method of Threshold Bible Study is rooted in the classical tradition of *lectio divina,* an ancient yet contemporary means for reading the Scriptures reflectively and prayerfully. Reading and interpreting the text (*lectio*) is followed by reflective meditation on its message (*meditatio*). This reading and reflecting flows into prayer from the heart (*oratio* and *contemplatio*).

This ancient method assures us that Bible study is a matter of both the mind and the heart. It is not just an intellectual exercise to learn more and be able to discuss the Bible with others. It is, more importantly, a transforming experience. Reflecting on God's word, guided by the Holy Spirit, illumines the mind with wisdom and stirs the heart with zeal.

Following the personal Bible study, Threshold Bible Study offers a method for extending *lectio divina* into a weekly conversation with a small group. This communal experience will allow participants to enhance their appreciation of the message and build up a spiritual community (*collatio*). The end result will be to increase not only individual faith, but also faithful witness in the context of daily life (*operatio*).

Through the spiritual disciplines of Scripture reading, study, reflection, conversation, and prayer, you will experience God's grace more abundantly as your life is rooted more deeply in Christ. The risen Jesus said: "Listen! I am standing at the door, knocking; if you hear my voice and open the door, I will come in to you and eat with you, and you with me" (Rev 3:20). Listen to the Word of God, open the door, and cross the threshold to an unimaginable dwelling with God!

SUGGESTIONS FOR INDIVIDUAL STUDY

• Make your Bible reading a time of prayer. Ask for God's guidance as your read the Scriptures.

• Try to study daily, or as often as possible according to the circumstances of your life.

• Read the Bible passage carefully, trying to understand both its meaning and its personal application as you read. Some persons find it helpful to read the passage aloud.

• Read the passage in another Bible translation. Each version adds to your understanding of the original text.

• Allow the commentary to help you comprehend and apply the scriptural text. The commentary is only a beginning, not the last word on the meaning of the passage.

• After reflecting on each question, write out your responses. The very act of writing will help you clarify your thoughts, bring new insights, and amplify your understanding.

• As you reflect on your answers, think about how you can live God's word in the context of your daily life.

• Conclude each daily lesson by reading the prayer and continuing with your own prayer from the heart.

• Make sure your reflections and prayers are matters of both the mind and the heart. A true encounter with God's word is always a transforming experience.

• Choose a word or a phrase from the lesson to carry with you throughout the day as a reminder of your encounter with God's life-changing word.

• Share your learning experience with at least one other person whom you trust for additional insights and affirmation. The ideal way to share learning is in a small group that meets regularly.

SUGGESTIONS FOR GROUP STUDY

• Meet regularly; weekly is ideal. Try to be on time and make attendance a high priority for the sake of the group. The average group meets for about an hour.

• Open each session with a prepared prayer, a song, or a reflection. Find some appropriate way to bring the group from the workaday world into a sacred time of graced sharing.

• If you have not been together before, name tags are very helpful as a group begins to become acquainted with the other group members.

• Spend the first session getting acquainted with one another, reading the Introduction aloud, and discussing the questions that follow.

• Appoint a group facilitator to provide guidance to the discussion. The role of facilitator may rotate among members each week. The facilitator simply keeps the discussion on track; each person shares responsibility for the group. There is no need for the facilitator to be a trained teacher.

• Try to study the six lessons on your own during the week. When you have done your own reflection and written your own answers, you will be better prepared to discuss the six scriptural lessons with the group. If you have not had an opportunity to study the passages during the week, meet with the group anyway to share support and insights.

• Participate in the discussion as much as you are able, offering your thoughts, insights, feelings, and decisions. You learn by sharing with others the fruits of your study.

• Be careful not to dominate the discussion. It is important that everyone in the group be offered an equal opportunity to share the results of their work. Try to link what you say to the comments of others so that the group remains on the topic.

• When discussing your own personal thoughts or feelings, use "I" language. Be as personal and honest as appropriate and be very cautious about giving advice to others.

• Listen attentively to the other members of the group so as to learn from their insights. The words of the Bible affect each person in a different way, so a group provides a wealth of understanding for each member.

• Don't fear silence. Silence in a group is as important as silence in personal study. It allows individuals time to listen to the voice of God's Spirit and the opportunity to form their thoughts before they speak.

• Solicit several responses for each question. The thoughts of different people will build on the answers of others and will lead to deeper insights for all.

• Don't fear controversy. Differences of opinions are a sign of a healthy and honest group. If you cannot resolve an issue, continue on, agreeing to disagree. There is probably some truth in each viewpoint.

• Discuss the questions that seem most important for the group. There is no need to cover all the questions in the group session.

• Realize that some questions about the Bible cannot be resolved, even by experts. Don't get stuck on some issue for which there are no clear answers.

• Whatever is said in the group is said in confidence and should be regarded as such.

• Pray as a group in whatever way feels comfortable. Pray for the members of your group throughout the week.

Schedule for group study

Session 1: Introduction   Date: _____

Session 2: Lessons 1-6   Date: _____

Session 3: Lessons 7-12   Date: _____

Session 4: Lessons 13-18   Date: _____

Session 5: Lessons 19-24   Date: _____

Session 6: Lessons 25-30   Date: _____

For as often as you eat this bread and drink the cup,
you proclaim the Lord's death until he comes. 1 Cor 11:26

Eucharist

The whole of the Christian life comes together in the celebration of Eucharist. For the followers of Jesus, there is no greater act on earth. Whether to celebrate a royal wedding or to remember the victims of a national tragedy, for the canonization of a new saint or to establish a new missionary outpost in a foreign land, to implore protection for armies going into battle or in thanksgiving for a bountiful harvest, to celebrate a great feast day in a gothic cathedral or to remember the Lord's Day in a country church, followers of Jesus in every age obey the command of their master, "Do this in memory of me."

The church memorializes salvation history's most climactic moments through simple signs of bodily nourishment and universal gestures of hospitality and feasting. At the altar of Christ's sacrifice, the table of the Lord's Supper, the church expresses the solemn mystery of its faith: Christ has died, Christ is risen, Christ will come again. Celebrated in every epoch for two millennia and expressed in every culture scattered throughout the world, the Eucharist offers humanity's best to God. Eucharistic worship has inspired the finest works of human creativity, from the house churches of the early Christians to the solemn basilicas and splendid cathedrals of later centuries. Enhanced by architecture of diverse cultural styles, a rich tradition of painting, iconography, sculpture, and a diverse heritage of sacred music, the Eucharist has motivated artistic vision to honor the divine made flesh in sacramental mystery.

The richness of this ritual celebration is expressed through the different names it has been given. "The Lord's Supper" (1 Cor 11:20; Rev 19:9) recalls the founding meal that Jesus ate with his disciples on the eve of his sacrificial death and anticipates the wedding banquet of the Lamb in the future Jerusalem. "The breaking of the bread" (Acts 2:42) is the name given by the early Christians of Jerusalem for their communal worship in which they recognized the Risen Lord (Luke 24:35). "Holy Communion" expresses the unity we experience with Christ as the broken bread and cup of blessing become a communion in his body and blood (1 Cor 10:16–17). "The Divine Liturgy" evokes the fact that the public worship of the church finds its most intense expression in the eucharistic ritual, while "the Mass" brings to mind the sending forth (*missio*) that concludes the Eucharist, as participants are commissioned to serve Christ in the world. "Eucharist" comes from the Greek word *eucharistein*, "to give thanks" (1 Cor 11:24), recalling the Jewish blessings that give thanks for God's work of creation, redemption, and sanctification. Each name evokes diverse aspects of the unlimited treasure of the Christian Eucharist.

Eucharist, the center of the church's life, somehow seems to say it all. It says in a hundred different ways: this is who we are, and this is who God is. It can make us sorrowful and joyful, enthusiastic and silent, committed and awestruck all at once. When we look at Eucharist in all its rich fullness, we can rekindle within ourselves eucharistic amazement and wonder at this great gift God has given us in his Son Jesus.

Reflection and discussion

• What thoughts and emotions come to mind in association with Eucharist?

humility

• Has Eucharist lost its amazement for me? In what ways can I rekindle wonder at this divine gift?

Holy and Living Sacrifice of the New Covenant

The Eucharist is permanently marked by the climactic event of Christ's passion and death. He instituted the Eucharist on the night before his death on the cross and expressed the meaning of his saving death within the Eucharist. His words of self-offering assert that his death would be a sacrifice. His body is "given for you," and his blood is "poured out for you" (Luke 22:19–20), that is, offered in sacrifice. The Eucharist is Christ's supreme gift to his church: the gift of himself and the gift of his saving work.

The Lord's sacrifice is so decisive for humanity's salvation that he offered it and returned to the Father only after he had left us a means of sharing in it as if we had been present there. The sacrifice of Christ on the cross and the sacrifice of Christ in the Eucharist are one single sacrifice. Jesus Christ was offered "once for all" on the altar of his cross; yet that one sacrifice is made present anew wherever the Eucharist is celebrated until the end of the world. Since the work of Christ for our salvation cannot be confined to its historical time and place, we can say that Christ has offered and is always offering for us his saving sacrifice on the cross, which is sacramentally re-presented on the altars of his church across the world.

Paul taught, "As often as you eat this bread and drink the cup, you proclaim the Lord's death until he comes" (1 Cor 11:26). Though God has already accepted Christ's sacrifice in raising him to life, we continue to offer the memorial of Christ's sacrifice and share in the sacrificial meal because we want to share in the benefits of Christ's sacrifice. He is the living victim being continually offered to the Father as the one sacrifice for the world. In celebrating the Eucharist we are praying that the saving benefits of Christ's sacrifice have their effect in us, that in Christ we become a true offering to God. We are asking that, as the body of Christ, we be made a sacrifice to the Father, an offering that is truly acceptable because of the way we live as his people in union with Christ.

The high point of the life of the ancient Israelites was going up to Jerusalem to offer sacrifice in ceremonies that honor and glorify God. Some sacrifices were offered in reparation for sins, others in thanksgiving for specific blessings, and others to praise and worship God because he is God. Sacrifices involved offerings of animals as well as grains, bread, and wine. Holy meals were often part of the sacrificial ceremony and a way of sharing in it. The sacrifice consisted of the offering of the victim as well as the sharing of the meal. The sacrificial meal completed the sacrificial offering and gave participants a way to participate in the benefits of offering the sacrifice.

The New Testament teaches that the sacrifices of the old covenant were shadows or incomplete versions of the things to come. The total cleansing of sin, perfect thanksgiving, and complete worship of God would occur when Christ is both the priest who offers sacrifice and the sacrificial victim offered. The one, perfect sacrifice was accomplished as Christ willingly consecrated his whole life and gave himself completely as an offering to the Father out of love for the world. By raising his Son and bringing him into his heavenly presence, God received Christ's self-offering as a fully acceptable sacrifice. As the eternal high priest before God's throne, Christ is forever presenting his perfect sacrifice to the Father and interceding for us.

At the Last Supper, Jesus offered his body and blood in anticipation of what was to occur on the cross and as a means of sharing the blessings of that sacrifice with all who would take part in his church's Eucharist. When we partake of the Eucharist, we are asking to share in the saving benefits that come from the offering of Christ's body and blood on the cross, and we renew the sacrifice of the new covenant, deepening our covenant commitment and our bond in Christ.

The purpose of Christ's sacrifice was to make his whole church, the body of Christ, a holy offering, a sacrifice consecrated to God. In Christ, we belong to God and have been offered to him (Col 1:22). Through the Holy Spirit, we continually offer our lives in union with Christ to God. Paul urges us to make our lives sacrificial: "Present your bodies as a living sacrifice, holy and acceptable to God, which is your spiritual worship" (Rom 12:1). All of our prayers, works, joys, and sufferings can be presented to God along with the sacrifice of Christ as an acceptable offering to the Father. We thus become "a holy

order of the Levites the priestly tribe

priesthood, to offer spiritual sacrifices acceptable to God through Jesus Christ" (1 Pet 2:5). By consciously making our lives a sacrifice to God, we express our desire to honor God and acknowledge him as our God. In this way, the offering of the church through all generations is offered in union with the eucharistic sacrifice of Christ on the altar.

Reflection and discussion

• In what way are the sacrifice of Christ on the cross and the sacrifice of Christ in the Eucharist the same sacrifice?

the "real presence", not bound by time or space
offered & offered each time the Eucharist
is said. a living sacrifice
"one sacrifice" once & for all
self-giving surrender

• How can I offer my life more consciously to the Father in union with the sacrifice of Christ?

awareness, conscious discipline
surrender
yes, (doing & saying)

Real and Living Presence of Christ

The Eucharist makes present not only the mystery of the Lord's passion and death, but also the crown of his sacrifice, the resurrection. Because he is the living and risen Lord, Christ can become our eternal sacrifice and our life-giving bread for the world. When we celebrate Eucharist, the Risen Lord is truly and sacramentally present for us. He gives us his whole being; his presence is real, substantial, and whole. The one who loved us on the cross, the one who has given himself completely, is here for us. The constant faith of the church confirms, though our senses suggest otherwise, that in the most blessed sacrament of the Eucharist, Christ is truly present—body and blood, soul and divinity. Human reason surely experiences its limitations before this mystery of God's love.

The real presence of the Lord in the Eucharist is a conclusion consistent with the biblical revelation about God who manifests himself as God-with-us. The elusive glory of God came and went throughout the narratives of the Hebrew Scriptures, but now that divine presence manifests itself in real, bodily reality, permanently with us. Throughout salvation history, God's universal and external presence became increasingly personal and interior in us. The Eucharist is the final step in the long path of God's "descent" into the human condition: creation, revelation, incarnation, Eucharist.

The Eucharist is the expression of the paschal mystery of Christ's death and resurrection, but it is equally an expression of the incarnation, God's becoming flesh among us. It is the memorial of what Christ did for us as well as the real presence of the Word made flesh. In the incarnation the Word became flesh (John 1:14); in the Eucharist he has given us his flesh to eat (John 6:52–56). It is as the Word made flesh that Jesus died, rose, is exalted, and is now present to us in this sacrament. In the Eucharist the two great mysteries of incarnation and redemption come together and offer us eternal life.

The real presence of Christ in the Eucharist means that he is objectively present with us, in contrast to something that is only mentally present to us, like an idea or memory. We may be low in faith, lacking in desire, or inattentive, but Christ is truly there. In Eucharist we relive the experience of the disciples who came to experience the presence of the risen Lord when they broke bread with him at Emmaus: "Their eyes were opened and they recognized him" (Luke 24:31). When grace opens our interior eyes with insight and we understand more deeply the wondrous mystery of Christ's living presence in Eucharist, we recognize the one who wants to be received by us with hearts overflowing with reverence and devotion.

Jesus Christ gives himself to us in bodily form, and so we must respond to him with bodily expression. There are lots of signs that indicate how deeply the eucharistic presence of Christ is felt in a faith community. The church's liturgy includes numerous bodily gestures. With hymns of praise, words of thanksgiving, profound silence, burning candles and wafting incense, humble bows and genuflections, standing and kneeling, the church adores her saving Lord. The church also venerates Christ's eucharistic presence outside the liturgy, through reservation of the sacrament in the tabernacle, exposition of the sacrament for adoration and prayerful contemplation, and eucharistic processions. The eucharistic mystery remains present outside the liturgy because Christ is always giving himself. In all of these ways people express their faith in Christ's living presence, but the greatest sign of a faithful, eucharistic community is demonstrating the presence of Christ alive in the world through bodily expressions of his self-giving love.

A nonchristian once said: "If I could believe as you believe that God is really there on the altar, I think I would fall on my knees and stay there forever." Though we must not remain on our knees because God has given us responsibilities in the world, we can maintain an orientation toward the eucharistic presence of Christ. We can continue to adore the Lord in our hearts as we work, travel, and care for our families. The real presence is not only a personal gift but a responsibility we have to the world around us. When the disciples at Emmaus "recognized" the presence of Christ, they hastened to tell the other disciples. When we recognize our eucharistic Lord, we no longer want to live for ourselves but for him, and the world around us becomes our field of mission.

Reflection and discussion

• In what way is the real presence of Christ in the Eucharist consistent with the history of God's revelation of himself?

God's "descent" into the human condition. Creation, revelation, incarnation

• What can deepen my faith in the real presence of Christ in the Eucharist?

A life lived as Christ is present.

Feasting at the Table of the Lord

The Eucharist is both a vertical event, making present Christ's sacrifice on the cross, and a horizontal event, uniting his community at a sacred banquet of communion in his body and blood. The place around which disciples gather is, at the same time, the altar of Christ's sacrifice and the table of the Lord. Christ himself is both the sacrificial victim offered for our redemption and food from heaven as he gives himself for our nourishment.

The sacrifice at the altar and the holy meal around the table are presented in the New Testament as a new Passover. The ancient Passover of Israel took place in two moments: the sacrificial offering of the lamb in the temple and the communal supper gathered around the table. John's gospel emphasizes that Jesus is the Lamb of the New Passover, sacrificed on the cross so that the food and drink of his flesh and blood might bring eternal life to all believers. The other gospels focus on the institution of the Eucharist at the Passover supper. The bread and wine at the table become the body of Christ broken for us and the blood of the new covenant.

Eucharistic sacrifice is directed toward the union of disciples with Christ through communion. In receiving the Lord's body and blood in communion, the saving effect of the sacrifice is fully realized. Christ himself becomes our nourishment for the journey, and food for our pilgrimage through life. What earthly food produces in our bodily life, communion in Christ's sacramental presence achieves in our spiritual life. In the most intimate union imaginable in our physical lives, Christ gives his very self to us to be consumed and digested, so that we become one with him and share in his very life. Christ assures us: "Those who eat my flesh and drink my blood abide in me, and I in them" (John 6:56).

At the table of Eucharist we look back to the Last Supper and the passion of Christ, and we also look forward to the banquet of that new world God wants to create. The memory of the past, the presence of grace, and the expectation of the glorious future come together in the eternal, eucharistic moment. God wants to make the world alive in a new way, like he did for Jesus on the first day of the week. The Eucharist is a sure pledge of the world to come; it is an anticipation of the goal, a foretaste of the fullness of joy promised by Christ. Celebrating Eucharist plants a seed of hope in our daily commitment to the work we do in this life and allows us a glimpse of heaven on earth. It offers us a deeper sense of responsibility for creation, obliging us to seek God's will on earth, committing us to transforming the world in harmony with God plan.

As we are nourished by Christ's body and blood, we are filled with his Holy Spirit. Jesus lives within us, as though he's put his breath inside us. The Holy Spirit makes us want to be like Jesus, led by his Spirit, wanting to do things his way. Celebrating Eucharist proclaims to the world that forgiveness has been given and death has been defeated. We don't have to wait until after death to receive eternal life; we already possess it in our sacramental union with Christ (John 6:54). The whole world has become a different place, and we are already living in the new world to come. In celebrating the Eucharist, we are united to the heavenly liturgy and become a part of that great multitude of angels, apostles, martyrs, and saints, worshiping God. The expectation of "a new heaven and a new earth" (Rev 21:1) assures us that the banquet to come will be a communion between God and a creation renewed in his love.

Reflection and discussion

• What do I really experience as I feast at the table of the Lord?

varies from peace, joy, humility, sadness contrition

• In what way does the Eucharist offer us a glimpse of our hope for the future?

future holds the permanence of living with Christ and doing his will joyously

Exploring the Biblical Sources of Eucharist

From Old Testament archetypes, to Jesus and his church, to our own sacramental life—this is the type of connection we will trace in this study as we deepen our understanding of the rich biblical roots of Eucharist. It may seem surprising that a study of Eucharist would spend so much time focusing on the Old Testament. But we will be following the lead of the church's earliest theologians, who built our eucharistic understanding around the insight that the sacraments fulfill God's ancient promises. The people and events of the Old Testament are "types" or "foreshadowings" of Christian realities.

In the early church, the catechumens were baptized and anointed at the Easter Vigil and participated in the Eucharist for the first time. While they had learned the stories of the Old and New Testaments during their time of preparation, only in light of the Easter sacraments were they able to understand the deeper spiritual realities these stories communicated. A period of reflective instruction after Easter helped the new Christians understand the sacraments they had received in light of the ancient Scriptures.

We too will follow the gradual, reflective process of the early church as we reflect on these sacred texts of the Bible and use them to deepen our understanding of the Eucharist we experience. This study will root our understanding of the Eucharist deeply and thoroughly in sacred Scripture. Encountering the biblical sources for the Eucharist can inspire fidelity to the church's tradition and evoke new appreciation for the Eucharist we already know from our experience. These scriptural texts will have done their work in us when we present the sacrifice of Christ to the Father with greater faith and when we receive communion knowing that Christ will transform our lives as we live in him with greater faith, hope, and love.

Prayer

Crucified and Risen Lord, you have given to your church the great gift of Eucharist as a memorial of our redemption. Give me a new appreciation of the meaning of your Eucharist as I study your revelation and reflect on the sacred Scriptures. Human senses fail and human reason falters when confronted with this sacrament of your divine love. Give me eyes to recognize your living presence as you give me your body to eat and your blood to drink, and deepen my faith in the holy mystery of your Eucharist.

SUGGESTIONS FOR FACILITATORS, GROUP SESSION 1

1. If the group is meeting for the first time, or if there are newcomers joining the group, it is helpful to provide nametags.

2. Ask the participants to introduce themselves and tell the group a bit about themselves. You may want to ask one or more of these introductory questions:
   • What drew you to join this group?
   • What is your biggest fear in beginning this Bible study?
   • What do you most hope to gain in this study?

3. Distribute the books to the members of the group.

4. You may want to pray this prayer as a group:

Come upon us, Holy Spirit, to enlighten and guide us as we begin this study of the holy Eucharist. You inspired the writers of the Scriptures to reveal the Eucharist in many different ways throughout the history of salvation. Now stir our minds and our hearts to long for the sacrificial and saving presence of Christ in the blessed sacrament of the altar and to penetrate ever more deeply into the mystery of this great gift of Christ to his church. Motivate us to read the Scriptures, give us a love for God's word, and enflame our hearts so that we may reflect on that word and understand its truths. Bless us during this session and throughout the coming week with the fire of your love.

5. Read the Introduction aloud, pausing at each question for discussion. Group members may wish to write down the insights of the group as each question is discussed. Encourage several members of the group to respond to each question.

6. Don't feel compelled to finish the complete Introduction during the session. It is better to allow sufficient time to talk about the questions raised than to rush to the end. Group members may read any remaining sections on their own after the group meeting.

8. Instruct group members to read the first six lessons on their own during the six days before the next group meeting. They should write out their own answers to the questions as preparation for next week's group discussion.

9. Fill in the date for each group meeting under "Schedule for Group Study."

10. Conclude by praying aloud together the prayer at the end of the Introduction.

Unlike the other high priests, he has no need to offer sacrifices day after day, first for his own sins, and then for those of the people; this he did once for all when he offered himself. Heb 7:27

Another Priest Like Melchizedek

GENESIS 14:18–20 ¹⁸*And King Melchizedek of Salem brought out bread and wine; he was priest of God Most High. ¹⁹He blessed him and said, "Blessed be Abram by God Most High, maker of heaven and earth; ²⁰and blessed be God Most High, who has delivered your enemies into your hand!" And Abram gave him one tenth of everything.*

HEBREWS 7:11–28 ¹¹*Now if perfection had been attainable through the levitical priesthood—for the people received the law under this priesthood— what further need would there have been to speak of another priest arising according to the order of Melchizedek, rather than one according to the order of Aaron? ¹²For when there is a change in the priesthood, there is necessarily a change in the law as well. ¹³Now the one of whom these things are spoken belonged to another tribe, from which no one has ever served at the altar. ¹⁴For it is evident that our Lord was descended from Judah, and in connection with that tribe Moses said nothing about priests.*

¹⁵*It is even more obvious when another priest arises, resembling Melchizedek, ¹⁶one who has become a priest, not through a legal requirement concerning physical descent, but through the power of an indestructible life. ¹⁷For it is attested of him,*

12

"You are a priest forever,

according to the order of Melchizedek."

[18] *There is, on the one hand, the abrogation of an earlier commandment because it was weak and ineffectual* [19] *(for the law made nothing perfect); there is, on the other hand, the introduction of a better hope, through which we approach God.*

[20] *This was confirmed with an oath; for others who became priests took their office without an oath,* [21] *but this one became a priest with an oath, because of the one who said to him,*

"The Lord has sworn and will not change his mind,

'You are a priest forever'"— [22] *accordingly Jesus has also become the guarantee of a better covenant.*

[23] *Furthermore, the former priests were many in number, because they were prevented by death from continuing in office;* [24] *but he holds his priesthood permanently, because he continues forever.* [25] *Consequently he is able for all time to save those who approach God through him, since he always lives to make intercession for them.*

[26] *For it was fitting that we should have such a high priest, holy, blameless, undefiled, separated from sinners, and exalted above the heavens.* [27] *Unlike the other high priests, he has no need to offer sacrifices day after day, first for his own sins, and then for those of the people; this he did once for all when he offered himself.* [28] *For the law appoints as high priests those who are subject to weakness, but the word of the oath, which came later than the law, appoints a Son who has been made perfect forever.*

The mysterious figure of Melchizedek makes only a brief appearance in the Old Testament. He is both a king and a priest: the king of Salem and a priest of God Most High (Gen 14:18). The short narrative is found in the stories of Abraham in the book of Genesis. When Abram was returning from battle, Melchizedek met him at the gates of his city (traditionally understood to be Jerusalem, Ps 76:2). Melchizedek brought out bread and wine for a victory feast and, as a priest, pronounced a blessing upon Abram, which praised God as creator and savior (Gen 14:19–20).

Melchizedek is mentioned only one other time in the Hebrew Scriptures. In a royal psalm extolling the Davidic ruler of Jerusalem, it is said of the king, "You are a priest forever according to the order of Melchizedek" (Ps 110:4). Like Melchizedek, the Canaanite king of pre-Israelite Jerusalem, the Israelite king is reminded that he is both priest and king, chief mediator between God and the people. Melchizedek's service as priest to Abram immortalized him as the model of sacred kingship and a foreshadowing of the messiah to come.

The Letter to the Hebrews used the figure of Melchizedek to reflect on the priesthood of Jesus Christ. The author compares the old priesthood, the old law, the old covenant, and the old sacrifices with the new priesthood, the new law, the new covenant, and the one sacrifice of Jesus.

Like Melchizedek, the Son of God is a priest and a king, who offers bread and wine. In Jesus is established a new and more effective priesthood, replacing the levitical priesthood of the order of Aaron (Heb 7:11). These levitical priests died and had to be replaced by others; thus there were many priests of the old covenant (Heb 7:23). But Jesus is not of the tribe of Levi. He is unique and needs no replacement. His priesthood is eternal. Thus he is always alive, always making intercession for us, always mediating between us and God (Heb 7:24–25).

We now live in this new relationship with God through Christ. In the new covenant there is only one priest. The ministerial priesthood or ordained priests today and the universal priesthood of all Christian believers are both participations in the one priesthood of Christ. He is the perfect priest because he is holy and sinless (Heb 7:26). He is the perfect sacrifice because he offered himself (Heb 7:27). Because both the priest and the sacrificial victim are perfect, the sacrifice is eternally valid and effective. Jesus offered himself "once for all"—a sacrifice offered for all people and whose power is available to all who desire to receive it. We share in the one, perfect sacrifice of Christ when we unite our lives with Christ in Eucharist.

Reflection and discussion

• What are the characteristics of Melchizedek that make him a helpful prototype for understanding the work of Jesus?

• What does it mean to me to imagine Jesus as a priest? How does the fact that Jesus remains a priest forever make a difference in my trust before God?

• Why is there only one priest and only one sacrifice in the age of the new covenant?

it lives on eternally there is no need for another

• How can I unite the sacrifices and offerings of my life to the one, perfect sacrifice of Jesus Christ? Does his perfect sacrifice make my sacrifices seem less significant or more significant?

through Jesus
at His guidance
in His name
through (acknowledging) his power

Prayer

Perfect High Priest, you intercede for me as I share in the grace of your sacrifice. Help me to unite my daily prayers, works, joys, and sufferings to your cross, so that my life may also be a sacrificial offering for others.

Isaac said to his father Abraham, "Father!" And he said, "Here I am, my son." He said, "The fire and the wood are here, but where is the lamb for a burnt offering?" Abraham said, "God himself will provide the lamb for a burnt offering, my son." Gen 22:7–8

Abraham Offers His Beloved Son to God

GENESIS 22:1–19 ¹*After these things God tested Abraham. He said to him, "Abraham!" And he said, "Here I am." *²*He said, "Take your son, your only son Isaac, whom you love, and go to the land of Moriah, and offer him there as a burnt offering on one of the mountains that I shall show you."*

³*So Abraham rose early in the morning, saddled his donkey, and took two of his young men with him, and his son Isaac; he cut the wood for the burnt offering, and set out and went to the place in the distance that God had shown him.* ⁴*On the third day Abraham looked up and saw the place far away.* ⁵*Then Abraham said to his young men, "Stay here with the donkey; the boy and I will go over there; we will worship, and then we will come back to you."* ⁶*Abraham took the wood of the burnt offering and laid it on his son Isaac, and he himself carried the fire and the knife. So the two of them walked on together.* ⁷*Isaac said to his father Abraham, "Father!" And he said, "Here I am, my son." He said, "The fire and the wood are here, but where is the lamb for a burnt offering?"* ⁸*Abraham said, "God himself will provide the lamb for a burnt offering, my son." So the two of them walked on together.*

⁹*When they came to the place that God had shown him, Abraham built an*

altar there and laid the wood in order. He bound his son Isaac, and laid him on the altar, on top of the wood. ¹⁰Then Abraham reached out his hand and took the knife to kill his son. ¹¹But the angel of the Lord called to him from heaven, and said, "Abraham, Abraham!" And he said, "Here I am." ¹²He said, "Do not lay your hand on the boy or do anything to him; for now I know that you fear God, since you have not withheld your son, your only son, from me." ¹³And Abraham looked up and saw a ram, caught in a thicket by its horns. Abraham went and took the ram and offered it up as a burnt offering instead of his son. ¹⁴So Abraham called that place "The Lord will provide"; as it is said to this day, "On the mount of the Lord it shall be provided."

¹⁵The angel of the Lord called to Abraham a second time from heaven, ¹⁶and said, "By myself I have sworn, says the Lord: Because you have done this, and have not withheld your son, your only son, ¹⁷I will indeed bless you, and I will make your offspring as numerous as the stars of heaven and as the sand that is on the seashore. And your offspring shall possess the gate of their enemies, ¹⁸and by your offspring shall all the nations of the earth gain blessing for themselves, because you have obeyed my voice." ¹⁹So Abraham returned to his young men, and they arose and went together to Beer-sheba; and Abraham lived at Beer-sheba.

This account of Abraham's supreme test is the climactic episode of his long life and one of the Bible's most emotionally dramatic scenes. We can clearly imagine Abraham's heart breaking as God asks him to sacrifice Isaac—"your son, your only son Isaac, whom you love" (verse 2). This is the miraculous, promised child born to him and to Sarah in old age, their reward for a lifetime of waiting and faithfulness. Nothing God could ask of Abraham, not even his own life, would cost him more than the death of his beloved son.

The reader is told that God's command to Abraham was a "test" (verse 1). Though God's testing might seem to us unreasonable in light of our belief that God is all-knowing, yet throughout the Bible God is always engaged with his people—calling, leading, promising, providing, and yes, testing. God tests to determine who is serious about faith, to identify in whose lives he will fully be God, and to develop in his people certain desirable qualities for the life of faith. Abraham, knowing that he had received Isaac as a gift from God, is willing to surrender even this most precious treasure back to the giver. Like Job, Abraham is prepared to trust fully the God who gives and who takes away (Job 1:21).

We can only speculate about Abraham's interior emotions: Was he calm, angry, trusting, miserable, despairing? His actions are described with a verbal scarcity appropriate to the solemn silence that pervades the narrative. With only the sound of their sandals in the wilderness and the donkey's hooves, the long three-day trek allows time for somber reflection. Abraham could turn back at any time; his will was free; the burden of choice fell squarely on his shoulders. He knew that despite every reasonable impulse within him crying out to defy God's command, he must trustingly obey.

Nearing the mountain of sacrifice, Abraham told his attendants to wait with the donkey while he and Isaac climb the road to the divinely chosen place. "We will worship, and then we will come back to you" (verse 5). Is Abraham simply trying to conceal from Isaac the true purpose of the journey, or does he harbor a secret hope that indeed they may both return? Abraham took the wood for the sacrifice and laid it on the shoulders of his son (verse 6). Isaac, unaware, carried some of the instruments of his own destruction. "The two of them walked on together" (verses 6, 8)—Isaac in unsuspecting innocence and Abraham in unspeakable inner torment.

In the only words between the son and his father, Isaac asks, "The fire and the wood are here, but where is the lamb for a burnt-offering?" (verse 7). Is this penetrating query simply an obvious question, or, in a culture in which child sacrifice was not unknown, is a suspicion of the dreadful truth beginning to dawn on Isaac? Abraham's trusting words, "God himself will provide the lamb for a burnt-offering" (verse 8), expressed the hope that lay deep within him. Abraham knew that somehow the One who tested was also the One who provided.

The preparations for sacrifice are expressed in the starkest terms: Abraham built an altar, laid the wood upon it, bound his son, laid him on the altar, reached out his hand, and took the knife (verses 9-10). There is no dialogue; the anguished grief is beyond words. Since Abraham was elderly and Isaac was at least old enough to carry wood on his shoulders, surely the boy was strong enough to resist his father. But as Abraham was obedient to God, Isaac was obedient to his father and let himself be bound and placed on the altar.

At the moment Abraham raised his knife to slay his son, God's messenger called out to him and stayed his hand. "Now I know that you fear God, since you have not withheld your son, your only son, from me" (verses 11-12). Abraham's commitment to God had been put to the ultimate test, and he had shown himself wholehearted in his self-surrender to God's will. It is not that God's foreknowledge of Abraham's character was lacking; rather, for Abraham's sake, his inner potential had to be demonstrated in action.

Abraham interprets the fortuitous presence of a ram to mean that God desires a substitute sacrifice in place of his son (verse 13). We can't fully imagine the happiness as Isaac and Abraham watched the smoke of the offering ascend to God from the mountain that day. The perfect offering God sought from Abraham was faith, the willingness to trust and obey even at the ultimate cost.

Abraham called the place "The Lord will provide" (verse 14), a reminder to all Abraham's descendants that God truly does provide for the needs of those who trust him. Abraham's greatest challenge proves that the God who tests is also the God who provides. Throughout the history of salvation, God's people trusted that "God himself will provide the lamb" for sacrifice (verse 8). "The Lamb of God who takes away the sin of the world" (John 1:29) is God's perfect response to the faithful waiting of his people.

Abraham's willingness to offer up his son to God (verse 16) helps us to better understand God's work in his Son Jesus. God asked Abraham to do what God would do in offering up his only beloved Son on the cross. "He who did not withhold his own Son, but gave him up for us all" (Rom 8:32) is the same God who tested and provided for Abraham. The obedient offering of Abraham strengthened God's covenant with Abraham. The one who had proven faithful would have descendants as numerous as the stars of heaven and the sand on the seashore, and all the nations of the earth would be blessed because Abraham obeyed God's voice (verses 17-18). The sacrifice of Christ would initiate the new covenant, the perfect fulfillment of God's promise to bless all the people of the world.

Reflection and discussion

• What does God really want from Abraham? What has God taught me about myself through testing?

faith, obedience, trust that I am not always faithful

• What are the images in Abraham's binding of Isaac that foreshadow the sacrifice of Jesus on the cross?

Carry the wood
bound to the cross

• In the New Testament, Paul writes: "God is faithful, and he will not let you be tested beyond your strength, but with the testing he will also provide the way out so that you may be able to endure it" (1 Cor 10:13). How does Abraham's experience demonstrate the truth of Paul's words?

God allowed the testing and
provided the ram in the thicket

• In what way does the passion of Christ demonstrate that the God who tests is also the God who provides? How does the Eucharist show us that the God who tests also provides for our needs?

suffering of Christ, surrender
to God's will for Him, was the
sacrifice of love that opened the
new covenant btwn the people & God.
Eucharist, the living sacrifice, of which
we partake becomes the source of
our hope.

Prayer

God of Abraham and Isaac, you test your people so that they may develop faith and be identified as your own. Give me the strength to remain faithful, the trust to give my life to you, and the assurance that you provide for all my needs.

When your children ask you, "What do you mean by this observance?"
you shall say, "It is the passover sacrifice to the Lord,
for he passed over the houses of the Israelites in Egypt. Exod 12:26–27

Saved By the Blood of the Passover Lamb

EXODUS 12:1–14 ¹*The Lord said to Moses and Aaron in the land of Egypt:* ²*This month shall mark for you the beginning of months; it shall be the first month of the year for you.* ³*Tell the whole congregation of Israel that on the tenth of this month they are to take a lamb for each family, a lamb for each household.* ⁴*If a household is too small for a whole lamb, it shall join its closest neighbor in obtaining one; the lamb shall be divided in proportion to the number of people who eat of it.* ⁵*Your lamb shall be without blemish, a year-old male; you may take it from the sheep or from the goats.* ⁶*You shall keep it until the fourteenth day of this month; then the whole assembled congregation of Israel shall slaughter it at twilight.* ⁷*They shall take some of the blood and put it on the two doorposts and the lintel of the houses in which they eat it.* ⁸*They shall eat the lamb that same night; they shall eat it roasted over the fire with unleavened bread and bitter herbs.* ⁹*Do not eat any of it raw or boiled in water, but roasted over the fire, with its head, legs, and inner organs.* ¹⁰*You shall let none of it remain until the morning; anything that remains until the morning you shall burn.* ¹¹*This is how you shall eat it: your loins girded, your sandals on your feet, and your staff in your hand; and you shall eat it hurriedly. It is the passover of the Lord.* ¹²*For I will pass through the land of Egypt that night, and I will strike down every firstborn in* *the land of Egypt, both human beings and animals; on all the gods of Egypt I will execute judgments: I am the Lord.* [13] *The blood shall be a sign for you on the houses where you live: when I see the blood, I will pass over you, and no plague shall destroy you when I strike the land of Egypt.*

[14] *This day shall be a day of remembrance for you. You shall celebrate it as a festival to the Lord; throughout your generations you shall observe it as a perpetual ordinance.*

Historical narrative and ritual instructions for future generations are woven together throughout the book of Exodus. Here the story of the first Passover pauses to introduce directives for commemorating the event in the years to come. The celebration of Passover thus has a timeless quality. When the Israelites of future generations reenacted the Passover, it was not simply a recollection of a past event. Every time the Israelites memorialized the event of Passover throughout the centuries, the ritual made the saving power of the past event present again. The redeeming reality of the past became real in the ritual's timeless moment. It is as though all the past and future generations of Israel came together on this night around the Passover table to be reconstituted as the people of God.

The first Passover came at the climax of God's actions to free the Israelites from slavery in Egypt. Nine plagues of increasing severity had already befallen Egypt as punishment for Pharaoh's refusal to release the Israelites. The final and most terrible plague was the death of the first-born in every family, from Pharaoh's son down to the first-born of the animals. Only the Israelites would escape the plague, because their houses were to be marked by the redeeming blood of a lamb. God told the Israelites, "When I see the blood, I will pass over you" (verse 13). The sacrificed lamb substituted for the life of the first-born child, just as many centuries before the ram substituted for the offering of Isaac. God continued to fulfill the confident words of Abraham: "God himself will provide the lamb" (Gen 22:8).

The annual celebration of Passover consisted of two parts: first, the slaying of the lamb in the temple of Jerusalem, followed by the eating of the lamb around the family table. This combination of the sacrificial death of the lamb and the eating of the lamb's flesh in a ritual meal is called a communion sacrifice in Israel's tradition. As the people ate the sacrificial lamb, they shared more intimately in the offering of the sacrifice and offered their lives to God in the offering of the lamb. The yearly rite became the means for all of Israel's future generations to celebrate their covenant with the God who saved them from slavery and death. Thousands of years after the Exodus, Jewish parents would still explain the Passover ritual to their children: "It is because of what the Lord did for me when I came out of Egypt" (Exod 13:8). The meal became the personal connection of each generation back to the foundational events of their salvation.

At the time of Jesus, Passover was celebrated as a national feast in which many Jews would travel to Jerusalem. Each of the gospels emphasize that the final events of Jesus' life took place in the context of Passover. The gospels of Matthew, Mark, and Luke describe the Last Supper as a Passover meal that Jesus celebrated with his disciples at table on the night before his death. John's gospel, on the other hand, places the crucifixion and death of Jesus at the same time as the lambs were being sacrificed in Jerusalem's temple. For John, Jesus is truly the Lamb of God, the true Passover Lamb, who fulfills the ancient search of Israel's ancestors for the lamb that God would provide.

Reflection and discussion

• Paul describes Jesus as the sacrificed lamb of Passover (1 Cor 5:7). In what ways does the passion and death of Jesus fulfill the ancient Passover?

the pouring out of blood,
preparation and death
"in place of" as the lamb's blood was
in place of the first born, so Jesus'
blood was in place of our own!

• What were the two parts of the Passover sacrifice in ancient Israel? In what way does a communion sacrifice allow for the intimate involvement of all the people?

slaying
eating in shared company around
the table
Communion sacrifice, from individual
to community (family)

• How did the blood of the lamb redeem the Israelites in the first Passover? How does God redeem my life from slavery and death?

allowed them to leave, to be freed

by offering His love for us, gives us freedom to choose

• In what way do the gospels differ in connecting Passover to the final events of Jesus' life?

M—M—L: Passover was the meal as the last supper

Jn: The last supper the crucifixion and death of Jesus same time as the slaughter of the lamb's in preparation for the meal.

• What connections do I see between the Jewish Passover and the Christian Eucharist?

both were sacrifices that led to freedom, choice
both are rituals that live the past in real time now
both were gift from God
both were accepted + followed in faith in God's care of us

Prayer

God of freedom and life, you revealed your presence to Israel by freeing them from bondage and calling them to abundant life. Free me from the bondage to sin and death, and give me new life through the saving sacrifice of your Son, our Lord Jesus Christ.

Then the Lord said to Moses, "I am going to rain bread from heaven for you, and each day the people shall go out and gather enough for that day."

Exod 16:4

Bread in the Wilderness, Nourishment for the Journey

EXODUS 16:2–18 *²The whole congregation of the Israelites complained against Moses and Aaron in the wilderness. ³The Israelites said to them, "If only we had died by the hand of the Lord in the land of Egypt, when we sat by the fleshpots and ate our fill of bread; for you have brought us out into this wilderness to kill this whole assembly with hunger."*

⁴Then the Lord said to Moses, "I am going to rain bread from heaven for you, and each day the people shall go out and gather enough for that day. In that way I will test them, whether they will follow my instruction or not. ⁵On the sixth day, when they prepare what they bring in, it will be twice as much as they gather on other days." ⁶So Moses and Aaron said to all the Israelites, "In the evening you shall know that it was the Lord who brought you out of the land of Egypt, ⁷and in the morning you shall see the glory of the Lord, because he has heard your complaining against the Lord. For what are we, that you complain against us?" ⁸And Moses said, "When the Lord gives you meat to eat in the evening and your fill of bread in the morning, because the Lord has heard the complaining that you utter against him—what are we? Your complaining is not against us but against the Lord."

⁹*Then Moses said to Aaron, "Say to the whole congregation of the Israelites, 'Draw near to the Lord, for he has heard your complaining.'"* ¹⁰*And as Aaron spoke to the whole congregation of the Israelites, they looked toward the wilderness, and the glory of the Lord appeared in the cloud.* ¹¹*The Lord spoke to Moses and said,* ¹²*"I have heard the complaining of the Israelites; say to them, 'At twilight you shall eat meat, and in the morning you shall have your fill of bread; then you shall know that I am the Lord your God.'"*

¹³*In the evening quails came up and covered the camp; and in the morning there was a layer of dew around the camp.* ¹⁴*When the layer of dew lifted, there on the surface of the wilderness was a fine flaky substance, as fine as frost on the ground.* ¹⁵*When the Israelites saw it, they said to one another, "What is it?" For they did not know what it was. Moses said to them, "It is the bread that the Lord has given you to eat.* ¹⁶*This is what the Lord has commanded: 'Gather as much of it as each of you needs, an omer to a person according to the number of persons, all providing for those in their own tents.'"* ¹⁷*The Israelites did so, some gathering more, some less.* ¹⁸*But when they measured it with an omer, those who gathered much had nothing over, and those who gathered little had no shortage; they gathered as much as each of them needed.*

Shortly after leaving the slavery of Egypt, the Israelites complained against Moses and Aaron in the wilderness. Presumably they had consumed the provisions with which they left Egypt, and after traveling for a while in the wilderness, they were hungry. Their "complaining" is mentioned seven times in these verses (verses 2, 7–12). They had not yet learned where to turn for their source of life, so they looked back with longing to the table of Pharaoh. Facing all the uncertainties that a liberated life with God entails, the Israelite community regretted their redemption and wanted to return to the security of their former bondage.

Remarkably the complaints of God's people become the springboard for God's display of grace. God promises meat in the evening and bread in the morning so that his people might come to know Yahweh as the one who generously sustains their lives (verses 8, 12). When the Israelites abide with God in freedom and rely on God's providence, they realize that God provides them with daily bread and all that they need for life.

When the Israelites saw the thin flaky manna on the ground, they did not know what it was. Moses responded to their inquiry: "It is the bread that the

Lord has given you to eat" (verse 15). The manna in the wilderness became the daily supply of food throughout Israel's sojourn in the desert: "The Israelites ate manna for forty years, until they came to a habitable land" (Exod 16:35). As we might expect, God's gift of manna offered much more than food; it became a means of instruction. The people were told to gather only their daily portion of manna. They were to gather it in such a way that everyone had enough to eat and no one had too little. They could not store up a supply, except before the Sabbath, when they were to gather twice as much so they need not work on the Sabbath itself. Their diet of manna compelled the Israelites to recognize their dependence on God to give them "daily bread."

Later Jewish writing suggested that in the age to come the manna would reappear. Jesus looked back on this Exodus tradition when he was teaching his followers about the gift of his life for them. Following the multiplication of the loaves and fish to feed the hungry masses, the crowd wanted Jesus to perform some new sign like the "bread from heaven" that God gave his people in the desert. Jesus explained that his Father gives "the true bread from heaven," which gives life to the world (John 6:30–34). When his disciples urged, "Sir, give us this bread always," Jesus declared to them, "I am the bread of life. Your ancestors ate the manna in the wilderness, and they died. This is the bread that comes down from heaven, so that one may eat of it and not die. I am the living bread that came down from heaven. Whoever eats of this bread will live forever; and the bread that I will give for the life of the world is my flesh" (John 6:48–51).

Reflection and discussion

• What did God want to teach his people by supplying them with manna in the wilderness?

reliance, dependence on Him

• Why did God give the Israelites only one day's supply of manna at a time? How easy would I find it to trust God to provide just enough food for each day's needs?

> *to test?*
> *to reinforce that everyday God gives us what we need for life.*

• What aspects of God's gift of manna prefigure Christ's gift of the Eucharist?

> *manna - gift from God*
> *Jesus - " " "*
> *bread }*
> *wine } body + blood, our food for the journey*

• In what way is Jesus Christ the "true bread from heaven" which gives life for the world?

> *came down from heaven, eat of His flesh will live forever*
> *grace*
> *hope*
> *presence.*
> *self-sacrifice*

Prayer

God of Moses and Aaron, you gave your people bread from heaven in the wilderness. Teach me to trust in you for my daily needs and to believe that you are the bread that comes down from heaven and gives life to the world.

Moses took the blood and dashed it on the people, and said, "See the blood of the covenant that the Lord has made with you in accordance with all these words." Exod 24:8

The Blood of the Ancient Covenant

EXODUS 24:3–8 *³Moses came and told the people all the words of the Lord and all the ordinances; and all the people answered with one voice, and said, "All the words that the Lord has spoken we will do." ⁴And Moses wrote down all the words of the Lord. He rose early in the morning, and built an altar at the foot of the mountain, and set up twelve pillars, corresponding to the twelve tribes of Israel. ⁵He sent young men of the people of Israel, who offered burnt offerings and sacrificed oxen as offerings of well-being to the Lord. ⁶Moses took half of the blood and put it in basins, and half of the blood he dashed against the altar. ⁷Then he took the book of the covenant, and read it in the hearing of the people; and they said, "All that the Lord has spoken we will do, and we will be obedient." ⁸Moses took the blood and dashed it on the people, and said, "See the blood of the covenant that the Lord has made with you in accordance with all these words."*

JEREMIAH 31:31–34 *³¹The days are surely coming, says the Lord, when I will make a new covenant with the house of Israel and the house of Judah. ³²It will not be like the covenant that I made with their ancestors when I took them by the hand to bring them out of the land of Egypt—a covenant that they broke, though I was their husband, says the Lord. ³³But this is the covenant that I will make with* *the house of Israel after those days, says the Lord: I will put my law within them, and I will write it on their hearts; and I will be their God, and they shall be my people. ³⁴No longer shall they teach one another, or say to each other, "Know the Lord," for they shall all know me, from the least of them to the greatest, says the Lord; for I will forgive their iniquity, and remember their sin no more.*

In the ancient Middle East, a covenant was a solemn and binding agreement. It was the kind of union that bound a king to his people or warring tribes in a lasting alliance. The pledge of covenant is used throughout the Old Testament to describe the special relationship between God and his people, an agreement involving both promises and obligations. At Mount Sinai, the covenant established a permanent commitment between God and the Israelites that would forever affect their history. The Israelites were assured of God's blessings, and they promised to obey his word and live as a priestly people.

The solemn ceremonies accompanying the making of a covenant suggest its seriousness and permanence. In ratifying the covenant at Sinai, Moses built an altar and sealed the covenant with the blood of sacrifice. He dashed half of the blood of the sacrificial animals upon the altar, representing God, and, after reading the book of the covenant, he dashed the other half upon the people (Exod 24:6–8). The blood is the seal and pledge of the covenant, establishing a community of life between God and his people. This blood bond is described by Moses as "the blood of the covenant that the Lord has made with you."

Though renewals of Israel's covenant with God are recorded throughout the Scriptures at critical junctures of history, God's people often broke the covenant with God. Yet despite their infidelity, God remained faithful and promised to establish a "new covenant" with them in the coming age. The prophet Jeremiah foresaw a new covenant that would be written on the heart and not on stone tablets like the covenant at Sinai, a relationship based on internal conviction rather than external obligation. In this new relationship, God's people would all know him and experience forgiveness of their sins (Jer 31:33–34).

The sacrificial love and death of Jesus Christ transformed the ancient relationship between God and his people. The New Testament accounts of the Last Supper connect the covenant with the shedding of Christ's blood. The gospel of Mark describes the cup as "my blood of the covenant, which is poured out for many" (Mark 14:24), and Matthew's gospel follows the same words with the addition of the phrase "for the forgiveness of sins" (Matt

26:28). The accounts of Paul and Luke specify that the covenant ratified on the cross is the new covenant anticipated by Jeremiah: "This cup is the new covenant in my blood" (1 Cor 11:25; Luke 22:20). The writers contrast the new covenant in Christ's blood with all other preceding covenants. The church's celebration of the Eucharist, in which the blood of Christ is offered upon the altar and given to the people to drink, is the renewal of the covenant ratified upon the cross. In celebrating the Eucharist, the church enters into the sacrifice of Christ whose blood ratifies the new and everlasting covenant.

Reflection and discussion

• What does the sacrificial blood dashed upon the altar and upon the people accomplish?

binds them God + people in a covenanted relationship promises + obligations

• What is the difference between the ancient covenant on Sinai and the new covenant foretold by Jeremiah?

external → ancient, follow the laws
internal → conviction of heart (

• In what way is participating in the Eucharist a commitment on my part? How serious am I in living up to my covenant obligations?

agreeing to accept and follow my internal conviction to God

Prayer

God of the covenant, in the desert you bound yourself forever to your people and renewed your promises throughout ancient history. Strengthen me through the Eucharist to hold fast to my commitment to you and renew your grace within me through the blood of Christ your Son.

He humbled you by letting you hunger, then by feeding you with manna,
with which neither you nor your ancestors were acquainted,
in order to make you understand that one does not live by bread alone,
but by every word that comes from the mouth of the Lord. Deut 8:3

Remember the Lord that He May Confirm His Covenant

DEUTERONOMY 8:2–18 *²Remember the long way that the Lord your God has led you these forty years in the wilderness, in order to humble you, testing you to know what was in your heart, whether or not you would keep his commandments. ³He humbled you by letting you hunger, then by feeding you with manna, with which neither you nor your ancestors were acquainted, in order to make you understand that one does not live by bread alone, but by every word that comes from the mouth of the Lord. ⁴The clothes on your back did not wear out and your feet did not swell these forty years. ⁵Know then in your heart that as a parent disciplines a child so the Lord your God disciplines you. ⁶Therefore keep the commandments of the Lord your God, by walking in his ways and by fearing him. ⁷For the Lord your God is bringing you into a good land, a land with flowing streams, with springs and underground waters welling up in valleys and hills, ⁸a land of wheat and barley, of vines and fig trees and pomegranates, a land of olive trees and honey, ⁹a land where you may eat bread without scarcity, where you will lack nothing, a land whose stones are iron and from whose hills you may mine copper. ¹⁰You shall eat your fill* *and bless the Lord your God for the good land that he has given you.*

¹¹ *Take care that you do not forget the Lord your God, by failing to keep his commandments, his ordinances, and his statutes, which I am commanding you today.* ¹² *When you have eaten your fill and have built fine houses and live in them,* ¹³ *and when your herds and flocks have multiplied, and your silver and gold is multiplied, and all that you have is multiplied,* ¹⁴ *then do not exalt yourself, forgetting the Lord your God, who brought you out of the land of Egypt, out of the house of slavery,* ¹⁵ *who led you through the great and terrible wilderness, an arid wasteland with poisonous snakes and scorpions. He made water flow for you from flint rock,* ¹⁶ *and fed you in the wilderness with manna that your ancestors did not know, to humble you and to test you, and in the end to do you good.* ¹⁷ *Do not say to yourself, "My power and the might of my own hand have gotten me this wealth."* ¹⁸ *But remember the Lord your God, for it is he who gives you power to get wealth, so that he may confirm his covenant that he swore to your ancestors, as he is doing today.*

When the Israelites were at the threshold of the promised land, God asked them to remember always how they hungered in the desert and how he fed them with the manna. Their sojourn in the wilderness was a learning experience that must never be forgotten. In the crucible of affliction, God tests and strengthens his people's hearts and wills. Though God's people would enter into a good and fruitful land where they would eat bread without scarcity, God wanted them to remember the wilderness and the feeding they enjoyed along the journey.

Though bread is essential for sustaining life, God tells his people, "One does not live by bread alone, but by every word that comes from the mouth of the Lord" (verse 3). God provided bread for his people in the wilderness as a humbling reminder of their dependence on him, but he used the gift of bread to teach them even more. Through the daily bread God taught them to live on every word that comes from God—the claims of God's covenant, the guidance of God's Scriptures, the comfort of God's promises. When they entered the plenteous land with abundant bread they were not to exalt themselves and boast, "My power and the might of my own hand have gotten me this wealth" (verse 17). The most significant lessons in the desert came through the most basic and universal form of human need—hunger. God humbled his people by letting them hunger, then by feeding them with manna (verses 3, 16).

The tradition of Israel praises God for the gift of heavenly food along their journey through the desert. The psalmist sings that the people asked with doubt, "Can God spread a table in the wilderness?" and God responded by giving them "manna to eat," "the grain of heaven," "the bread of angels" (Psalm 78:19, 24–25). The writer of the book of Wisdom praises God's care for his wandering people: "You give your people food of angels, and without your toil you supplied them from heaven with bread ready to eat" (Wis 16:20). Because the manna was such an important expression of God's daily care, the people in the desert were instructed to preserve some of the manna in the ark of the covenant as a reminder for coming generations (Exod 16:32–34).

The Eucharist is heavenly bread for our journey. Jesus tells us that he is "the living bread that came down from heaven" and that his flesh is bread for the life of the world (John 6:51). We cannot journey through life and live on bread alone, but we must live on every word that comes from the mouth of God. Jesus is the Word of God made flesh. The one who feeds on this Word of God made flesh will abide in him and enjoy eternal life (John 6:56–58).

Reflection and discussion

• What lessons for life did God teach his people in the wilderness?

Dependence on God

• Why are people unable to live on bread alone? What else is necessary for a whole and healthy life?

seeking God, through hunger
+ thirst
Community

• Why did God want his people to remember always their hunger and God's feeding them? When have I been fed by God while in hunger?

Mary, heart, pierced
pain in relationship

• How is "every word that comes from the mouth of the Lord" more nourishing than bread? How do I feed myself with God's word?

• Why is the Eucharist described as food for life's journey?

Prayer

Lord God, you test and humble your people by allowing us to hunger and then feeding us with the food we need. Teach me to depend on you for my daily bread and help me to hunger for the food that will nourish me forever. May Jesus, the bread of life, be for me the nourishing source of strength for my journey.

SUGGESTIONS FOR FACILITATORS, GROUP SESSION 2

1. If there are newcomers who were not present for the first group session, introduce them now.

2. You may want to pray this prayer as a group:

Lord God, you prepared the world for the great gift of Christ's Eucharist through-out the saving history of your people. Through the sacrifice of Abraham, our father in faith, the bread and wine offered by your priest Melchizedek, the redemptive blood of the Passover lamb, and the bread from heaven given to your people in the wilderness, you have shown us the richer meaning of the body and blood of Christ given as life for the world. Bless this gathering of hungry pilgrims, help us to listen to your word in the Scriptures, and give us a hunger for the bread of life through your Spirit alive among us.

3. Ask one or more of the following questions:
   • What was your biggest challenge in Bible study over this past week?
   • What did you learn about God's care for you this week?

4. Discuss lessons 1 through 6 together. Assuming that group members have read the Scripture and commentary during the week, there is no need to read it aloud. As you review each lesson, you might want to briefly summarize the Scripture passage of each lesson and ask the group what stands out most clearly about the commentary.

5. Choose one or more of the questions for reflection and discussion from each lesson to talk over as a group. You may want to ask group members which question was most challenging or helpful to them as you review each lesson.

6. Keep the discussion moving, but don't rush the discussion in order to complete more questions. Allow time for the questions that provoke the most discussion.

7. Remember that there are no definitive answers for these discussion questions. The insights of group members will add to the understanding of all. None of these questions requires an expert.

8. Instruct group members to complete lessons 7 through 12 on their own during the six days before the next group meeting. They should write out their own answers to the questions as preparation for next week's session.

9. Conclude by praying aloud together the prayer at the end of lesson 6, or any other prayer you choose.

"Get up and eat, otherwise the journey will be too much for you."
He got up, and ate and drank; then he went in the strength of that food for
forty days and forty nights to Horeb the mount of God. 1 Kings 19:7–8

Heavenly Nourishment for the Journey

1 KINGS 19:4–8 ⁴[Elijah] himself went a day's journey into the wilderness, and came and sat down under a solitary broom tree. He asked that he might die: "It is enough; now, O Lord, take away my life, for I am no better than my ancestors." ⁵Then he lay down under the broom tree and fell asleep. Suddenly an angel touched him and said to him, "Get up and eat." ⁶He looked, and there at his head was a cake baked on hot stones, and a jar of water. He ate and drank, and lay down again. ⁷The angel of the Lord came a second time, touched him, and said, "Get up and eat, otherwise the journey will be too much for you." ⁸He got up, and ate and drank; then he went in the strength of that food for forty days and forty nights to Horeb the mount of God.

2 KINGS 4:42–44 ⁴²A man came from Baal-shalishah, bringing food from the first fruits to the man of God: twenty loaves of barley and fresh ears of grain in his sack. Elisha said, "Give it to the people and let them eat." ⁴³But his servant said, "How can I set this before a hundred people?" So he repeated, "Give it to the people and let them eat, for thus says the Lord, 'They shall eat and have some left.'" ⁴⁴He set it before them, they ate, and had some left, according to the word of the Lord.

The journey of God's prophet Elijah in the wilderness echoes the journey of Moses and the Israelites. Elijah traveled for forty days and nights, a reminder of the forty-year trek of his ancestors, and came to the same mountain where God had revealed himself to his people many centuries before. To give him nourishment and strength for that long journey, God gave Elijah food and drink sent from heaven. This food in the wilderness, delivered by an angel of the Lord, was a gentle reminder of God's continual care for his people.

As the champion of Israel's covenant, Elijah had triumphed in his contest with the prophets of the god Baal. Yet, fleeing from the enraged pagan queen Jezebel, God's prophet was fearful, discouraged, and exiled from his home. Heading into the desert, he sought out a lonely place to die. He had given up, an isolated man under an isolated broom tree (1 Kings 19:4). But rather than permitting him to die, God not only provided him with food to sustain him but also sent him on another journey with a new commission (1 Kings 19:7). This story's interplay between human despair and God's call speaks to exiles of every age. God always offers us a new future in the solitary wilderness of fear and discouragement, and he offers us the spiritual nourishment to journey into that future with hope.

The second narrative shows another prophet of God, Elisha, providing food for a hungry crowd. The twenty loaves of barley and fresh ears of grain were the "first fruits" of the crop (2 Kings 4:42), the part usually offered in a thanksgiving sacrifice to God. Again, the power of God manifested through his prophet breaks into a situation of discouragement and hunger. The man who brought the loaves objected, "How can I set this before a hundred people," emphasizing the wonder of the event. Elisha insisted that the people would eat, trusting in the word of the Lord: "They shall eat and have some left" (2 Kings 4:43–44).

The early church told these feeding stories in conjunction with their memories of Jesus feeding the hungry crowds. When Jesus gave food to eat, the result was always abundant with plenty for all and food left over. He is good news for the exiled and hungry people of every age. His Eucharist is the heavenly food that keeps us going during times of fear, solitude, and discouragement.

Reflection and discussion

• In what ways have I experienced struggles like those of God's prophets?

• Where do I find the Lord's presence and strength during difficult times?

• In what ways do these accounts of God's prophets prefigure Christ's gift of the Eucharist? What do they tell us about the nature of Christ's gift?

Prayer

Lord God, you are the source of all that I have, and you provide for all my needs. In my fears, anxiety, and hunger, you give me food from heaven to satisfy my needs in abundance. Help me to trust in you for nourishment and strength.

On this mountain the Lord of hosts will make for all peoples a feast of rich food, a feast of well-aged wines, of rich food filled with marrow, of well-aged wines strained clear. Isa 25:6

The Banquet of God's Kingdom

ISAIAH 25:6–10

⁶*On this mountain the Lord of hosts will make for all peoples*
a feast of rich food, a feast of well-aged wines,
of rich food filled with marrow, of well-aged wines strained clear.
⁷*And he will destroy on this mountain*
the shroud that is cast over all peoples,
the sheet that is spread over all nations;
he will swallow up death forever.
⁸*Then the Lord God will wipe away the tears from all faces,*
and the disgrace of his people he will take away from all the earth,
for the Lord has spoken.
⁹*It will be said on that day,*
Lo, this is our God; we have waited for him, so that he might save us.
This is the Lord for whom we have waited;
let us be glad and rejoice in his salvation.
¹⁰*For the hand of the Lord will rest on this mountain.*

ISAIAH 55:1–5

¹*Ho, everyone who thirsts,*
   come to the waters;
and you that have no money,
   come, buy and eat!
Come, buy wine and milk
   without money and without price.
²*Why do you spend your money for that which is not bread,*
   and your labor for that which does not satisfy?
Listen carefully to me, and eat what is good,
   and delight yourselves in rich food.
³*Incline your ear, and come to me;*
   listen, so that you may live.
I will make with you an everlasting covenant,
   my steadfast, sure love for David.
⁴*See, I made him a witness to the peoples,*
   a leader and commander for the peoples.
⁵*See, you shall call nations that you do not know,*
   and nations that do not know you shall run to you,
because of the Lord your God, the Holy One of Israel,
   for he has glorified you.

In the ancient Middle East, table fellowship and feasting on rich food and wine expressed the fullness of life that God desires for his people. Likewise, hungering and thirsting expressed longing for God and yearning for his blessings. Rich imagery of banquets abounding in food and drink is found throughout the biblical literature to symbolize abundant life and the joy that comes with God's abiding presence.

The prophet Isaiah looked for a coming day when the world would be reborn and God's salvation would be complete and lasting. He used the image of a great banquet to convey these hopes and the promises of God. "A feast of rich food and well-aged wines" (Isa 25:6) enjoyed by all peoples on the mountain of Zion symbolizes the joyful abundance that Israel awaited in the age of the Messiah. That coming day of salvation would be a universal feast beyond comparison for all the nations. Tears of sorrow would be wiped away, and death would be swallowed up forever in unending joy and life (Isa 25:7–8). All people who have longed for salvation would recognize the God of Israel and exclaim, "Lo, this is our God; we have waited for him, so that he might save us" (Isa 25:9).

The second reading from Isaiah associates a feast of wine, bread, and rich food with God's "everlasting covenant" (Isa 55:1–3). The banquet is not limited to those of sufficient means or social standing. The only requirement is hunger and thirst. The covenant that God offered to his people through Abraham, Moses, and David, was ever expansive, reaching to "nations that do not know you" (Isa 55:5).

Isaiah's striking imagery of God's final banquet resounded down through the centuries and into the ministry of Jesus. His table fellowship with the poor, oppressed, and outcasts conveys the steadfast love of God, which seeks the lost. He is the one who "welcomes sinners and eats with them" (Luke 15:2). The Eucharist is the sacramental banquet in which we can celebrate even now the complete and eternal salvation that we will experience in God's kingdom. All who hunger and thirst can look forward to the messianic banquet that will celebrate the full union of Christ and his church at the end of time.

Reflection and discussion

• What aspects of a banquet make it a vivid image to express the presence and blessings of God?

• What other needs besides hunger and thirst does God promise to satisfy? What are my deepest needs?

• With whom did Jesus choose to dine? What does this tell me about my invitation to share his Eucharist?

• Why do the scriptures imagine life in God's future kingdom as a banquet?

overflowing — banquet

God draws us through hunger ——→ and feeds us with Eucharist

Prayer

Lord God of all the nations, you call all people to come to eat and drink at your table. Give me the desire to join your poor and oppressed people at the banquet of your kingdom.

*Those who eat of me will hunger for more,
and those who drink of me will thirst for more.* Sir 24:21

Come, Eat of My Bread and Drink of My Wine

PROVERBS 9:1–6

¹*Wisdom has built her house,
     she has hewn her seven pillars.*
²*She has slaughtered her animals, she has mixed her wine,
     she has also set her table.*
³*She has sent out her servant-girls, she calls
     from the highest places in the town,*
⁴*"You that are simple, turn in here!"
     To those without sense she says,*
⁵*"Come, eat of my bread
     and drink of the wine I have mixed.*
⁶*Lay aside immaturity, and live,
     and walk in the way of insight."*

SIRACH 24:19–22

¹⁹*"Come to me, you who desire me,
     and eat your fill of my fruits.*
²⁰*For the memory of me is sweeter than honey,
     and the possession of me sweeter than the honeycomb.*

²¹*Those who eat of me will hunger for more,*
     and those who drink of me will thirst for more.
²²*Whoever obeys me will not be put to shame,*
     and those who work with me will not sin."

In the wisdom literature of the Old Testament, Wisdom is personified and described as a manifestation of God's divinity present in the world. Proverbs describes Wisdom as begotten of God "before the beginning of the earth" (Prov 8:22–23). When God was planning the work of creation, Wisdom was beside him as an artisan or master worker and she was God's daily delight: "rejoicing before him always, rejoicing in his inhabited world, and delighting in the human race" (Prov 8:30–31). She is a divine presence mysteriously present in the world of nature and human experience, and she makes the extraordinary promise that true life is to be found in her: "Whoever finds me finds life" (Prov 8:35).

The book of Sirach continues this personification of Wisdom and describes her divine origins: "Before the ages, in the beginning he created me, and for all the ages I shall not cease to be" (Sir 24:9). Wisdom is a mysterious communication from God: "I came forth from the mouth of the Most High" (Sir 24:3). Though her throne was in the highest heavens, she sought a resting place on the earth. God chose Israel as her dwelling place; her resting place was to be in Jerusalem where she ministered before God in Zion's holy tent (the temple; Sir 24:4–12).

The description of living Wisdom in the Old Testament foreshadows the incarnate Word of God developed in John's gospel. Jesus is the Word, the complete communication from God in the flesh. The Word was "in the beginning with God," and "all things came into being through him" (John 1:1–3). Though he was of God and from God, "the Word became flesh and lived among us," literally he "dwelt in a tent among us" (John 1:14). Paul's writings also describe this completion of Old Testament Wisdom in Jesus Christ. He became for us "wisdom from God" (1 Cor 1:30). He is "the image of the invisible God, the firstborn of all creation" (Col 1:15). Old Testament Wisdom has become incarnate in Christ.

Proverbs describe Wisdom as sending forth an invitation to a great banquet, possibly a sacrificial feast in her seven-pillared temple. Through her servant-girls she issues forth the call, "Come, eat of my bread and drink of the wine I have mixed" (Prov 9:5). Those who accept the invitation to feast at the banquet of bread and wine enjoy the gift of life. In Sirach, Wisdom invites everyone to eat and drink of the riches she offers. Yet, when people taste of Wisdom, they hunger and thirst for more: "Those who eat of me will hunger for more, and those who drink of me will thirst for more" (Sir 24:21). Wisdom's banquet of life is most fully complete in Jesus, the living bread that gives eternal life (John 6:51). In him, the hungers of longing hearts can be satisfied completely, as he said, "Whoever comes to me will never be hungry, and whoever believes in me will never be thirsty" (John 6:35).

Reflection and discussion

• In what ways does the Old Testament description of Wisdom prepare for the New Testament description of the Word of God?

• In what ways is Wisdom described as a manifestation of God's presence in the world?

• What is the difference between the banquet Wisdom provides and Christ's food and drink?

• What is humanity's deepest hunger and thirst? What can finally satisfy those longings?

• In what way can God's presence in the world through Wisdom help me understand Christ's presence in Eucharist?

Prayer

Eternal God, you manifest yourself in the world as Holy Wisdom, the Word made flesh, the Bread of Life. You set a table before your people and invite the world to your banquet of life. Give me a deep longing for the food that satisfies my truest hungers and the drink that quenches my deepest thirsts.

He shall slaughter the goat of the sin offering that is for the people and bring its blood inside the curtain, and do with its blood as he did with the blood of the bull, sprinkling it upon the mercy seat and before the mercy seat. Lev 16:15

Atonement Through the Blood of Bulls and Goats

LEVITICUS 16:1–16 *¹The Lord spoke to Moses after the death of the two sons of Aaron, when they drew near before the Lord and died. ²The Lord said to Moses: Tell your brother Aaron not to come just at any time into the sanctuary inside the curtain before the mercy seat that is upon the ark, or he will die; for I appear in the cloud upon the mercy seat. ³Thus shall Aaron come into the holy place: with a young bull for a sin offering and a ram for a burnt offering. ⁴He shall put on the holy linen tunic, and shall have the linen undergarments next to his body, fasten the linen sash, and wear the linen turban; these are the holy vestments. He shall bathe his body in water, and then put them on. ⁵He shall take from the congregation of the people of Israel two male goats for a sin offering, and one ram for a burnt offering.*

⁶Aaron shall offer the bull as a sin offering for himself, and shall make atonement for himself and for his house. ⁷He shall take the two goats and set them before the Lord at the entrance of the tent of meeting; ⁸and Aaron shall cast lots on the two goats, one lot for the Lord and the other lot for Azazel. ⁹Aaron shall present the goat on which the lot fell for the Lord, and offer it as a sin offering; ¹⁰but the goat on which the lot fell for Azazel shall be presented alive before the Lord to make atonement over it, that it may be sent away into the wilderness to Azazel.

¹¹*Aaron shall present the bull as a sin offering for himself, and shall make atonement for himself and for his house; he shall slaughter the bull as a sin offering for himself.* ¹²*He shall take a censer full of coals of fire from the altar before the Lord, and two handfuls of crushed sweet incense, and he shall bring it inside the curtain* ¹³*and put the incense on the fire before the Lord, that the cloud of the incense may cover the mercy seat that is upon the covenant, or he will die.* ¹⁴*He shall take some of the blood of the bull, and sprinkle it with his finger on the front of the mercy seat, and before the mercy seat he shall sprinkle the blood with his finger seven times.*

¹⁵*He shall slaughter the goat of the sin offering that is for the people and bring its blood inside the curtain, and do with its blood as he did with the blood of the bull, sprinkling it upon the mercy seat and before the mercy seat.* ¹⁶*Thus he shall make atonement for the sanctuary, because of the uncleannesses of the people of Israel, and because of their transgressions, all their sins; and so he shall do for the tent of meeting, which remains with them in the midst of their uncleannesses.*

In Israel, as in most of the ancient world, blood was considered sacred because it is the bearer of life. The shedding of human blood was treated as a capital offense, but the shedding of animal blood was allowed, but only through a respectful ritual slaughter. The release of blood was seen as the release of the individual's life, and in animal sacrifice the shedding of the blood expressed the surrender of the life to God. In all animal sacrifices, the blood was an essential element: it was poured on the altar (Lev 1:5), placed on the doorframe of the houses (Exod 12:7), sprinkled upon the assembly (Exod 24:8), or sprinkled upon the mercy seat within the temple's inner sanctuary (Lev 16:15).

When the Israelites offered the animal sacrifices of the old covenant, the blood as bearer of life was given to God in atonement for the sins of humans. In a sin offering or burnt offering, the life of the animal victim substituted for the life of the sinful person. The one offering the sacrifice symbolically offered his or her own life to God, re-establishing the relationship with God. As God said in the book of Leviticus, "For the life of the flesh is in the blood; and I have given it to you for making atonement for your lives on the altar; for, as life, it is the blood that makes atonement" (Lev 17:11).

The most important sacrifices were the offering of the bull, the ram, and the goat on the annual Day of Atonement. On this one day of the year, the high priest entered the inner sanctum of Jerusalem's temple with a censer of hot coals and incense and the blood of the sacrificed animals. After engulfing the sanctuary with the haze of incense, the high priest sprinkled the sacrificial blood on the mercy seat, the sacred covering of the ark of the covenant where God was known to dwell, thereby bringing reconciliation between the Israelites and God (Lev 16:12–16).

The new covenant brought an end to the bloody sacrifices of Old Testament worship through "the precious blood of Christ" (1 Pet 1:19). For Paul, the offering of Christ on the cross is "a sacrifice of atonement by his blood" (Rom 3:25). Both the once-for-all death on the cross and the continually re-enacted Eucharist must be in Christ's blood. The presence of God and the place of atonement are not to be found at the mercy seat in the temple but on the hill of Golgotha and the altar of Eucharist. Since Christ sacrificed his life for us, we have been "justified by his blood" (Rom 5:9) and will be saved through him.

Reflection and discussion

• Why was blood such an essential element of the animal sacrifice of the old covenant?

• What was done with the blood in the Old Testament sacrifices? What did this symbolize?

• How does the ritual of the Day of Atonement express God's desire for a right relationship with his people? Why is this ritual of reconciliation important for the Israelites?

• Why is the blood of Christ at the heart of the sacrifice of the new covenant?

• How do the ancient sacrifices help me understand the atonement and reconciliation offered to me through Christ's Eucharist?

Prayer

Faithful God, the blood of ancient sacrifices expresses the serious rupture of human sin and the crucial importance of atonement with you. Reconcile me through the precious blood of Christ so that I may forever give you praise and worship.

**Indeed, under the law almost everything is purified with blood,
and without the shedding of blood there is no forgiveness of sins.** Heb 9:22

Forgiveness through the Blood of Christ

HEBREWS 9:1–28 ¹*Now even the first covenant had regulations for worship and an earthly sanctuary.* ²*For a tent was constructed, the first one, in which were the lampstand, the table, and the bread of the Presence; this is called the Holy Place.* ³*Behind the second curtain was a tent called the Holy of Holies.* ⁴*In it stood the golden altar of incense and the ark of the covenant overlaid on all sides with gold, in which there were a golden urn holding the manna, and Aaron's rod that budded, and the tablets of the covenant;* ⁵*above it were the cherubim of glory overshadowing the mercy seat. Of these things we cannot speak now in detail.*

⁶*Such preparations having been made, the priests go continually into the first tent to carry out their ritual duties;* ⁷*but only the high priest goes into the second, and he but once a year, and not without taking the blood that he offers for himself and for the sins committed unintentionally by the people.* ⁸*By this the Holy Spirit indicates that the way into the sanctuary has not yet been disclosed as long as the first tent is still standing.* ⁹*This is a symbol of the present time, during which gifts and sacrifices are offered that cannot perfect the conscience of the worshiper,* ¹⁰*but deal only with food and drink and various baptisms, regulations for the body imposed until the time comes to set things right.*

¹¹*But when Christ came as a high priest of the good things that have come, then*

through the greater and perfect tent (not made with hands, that is, not of this creation), [12] he entered once for all into the Holy Place, not with the blood of goats and calves, but with his own blood, thus obtaining eternal redemption. [13] For if the blood of goats and bulls, with the sprinkling of the ashes of a heifer, sanctifies those who have been defiled so that their flesh is purified, [14] how much more will the blood of Christ, who through the eternal Spirit offered himself without blemish to God, purify our conscience from dead works to worship the living God!

[15] For this reason he is the mediator of a new covenant, so that those who are called may receive the promised eternal inheritance, because a death has occurred that redeems them from the transgressions under the first covenant. [16] Where a will is involved, the death of the one who made it must be established. [17] For a will takes effect only at death, since it is not in force as long as the one who made it is alive. [18] Hence not even the first covenant was inaugurated without blood. [19] For when every commandment had been told to all the people by Moses in accordance with the law, he took the blood of calves and goats, with water and scarlet wool and hyssop, and sprinkled both the scroll itself and all the people, [20] saying, "This is the blood of the covenant that God has ordained for you." [21] And in the same way he sprinkled with the blood both the tent and all the vessels used in worship. [22] Indeed, under the law almost everything is purified with blood, and without the shedding of blood there is no forgiveness of sins.

[23] Thus it was necessary for the sketches of the heavenly things to be purified with these rites, but the heavenly things themselves need better sacrifices than these. [24] For Christ did not enter a sanctuary made by human hands, a mere copy of the true one, but he entered into heaven itself, now to appear in the presence of God on our behalf. [25] Nor was it to offer himself again and again, as the high priest enters the Holy Place year after year with blood that is not his own; [26] for then he would have had to suffer again and again since the foundation of the world. But as it is, he has appeared once for all at the end of the age to remove sin by the sacrifice of himself. [27] And just as it is appointed for mortals to die once, and after that the judgment, [28] so Christ, having been offered once to bear the sins of many, will appear a second time, not to deal with sin, but to save those who are eagerly waiting for him.

The history of God's people under the old covenant was about waiting and hoping, reaching forward toward an experience of God they could not grasp. They worshiped God in a transitory sanctuary, offering imperfect sacrifices through a provisional priesthood. The temple and all its rituals were only shadows, "sketches" (verse 23), or "copies" (verse 24), preparing for "the good things that have come" (verse 11) through the new covenant in Christ.

While the gospels depict the death of Jesus as a fulfillment of the Passover sacrifice, Hebrews focuses on the Day of Atonement, when the high priest entered the temple's inner sanctuary with a blood offering to atone for the people's sins (verse 7). Here we see Jesus not as the slain Lamb, but as the high priest who bears the atoning sacrifice of his own blood into the heavenly presence of God (verses 11-12). In the temple of Israel, the curtain was the ritual barrier that separated people from God's presence (verse 3). Christ, as the final and perfect high priest, "the mediator of a new covenant" (verse 15), has permanently pulled back the curtain of the sanctuary that shut us off from God. In him we can enter into an intimate encounter with God, personally know his loving forgiveness, and truly worship the living God.

The new covenant in Jesus Christ required both the death of Christ and the shedding of his blood. To explain the significance of Christ's death, the author shows that the Greek word for covenant can also mean "will" or "testament." Like a last will and testament, the covenant only takes effect when the person making the will dies (verses 16-17). The death of Jesus was the way we received "the promised eternal inheritance" (verse 15).

The first covenant was established with blood. The scroll of the law, the holy place, the vessels of worship, and God's people were sprinkled with the sacrificial blood (verses 18-21). Moses proclaimed, "This is the blood of the covenant" (verse 20). The author explains, "Under the law almost everything is purified with blood, and without the shedding of blood there is no forgiveness of sins" (verse 22). Thus the new covenant was established with the death of Christ and the shedding of his blood, the eternal sacrifice on the cross and the blood of the new and everlasting covenant.

Reflection and discussion

In what way is the Eucharist a pulling back of the barrier between us and God? How is the Eucharist for me an intimate experience of the presence of the living God?

In what way is the blood of the ancient covenant different from the blood of the new covenant? Why is blood vital for establishing a covenant?

What is the connection between our Eucharist and Christ's sacrificial offering to the Father in heaven?

Prayer

Eternal High Priest, you offered your blood on the cross once for all people. Through the Eucharist you offer us a lasting memorial through which we can continue to participate in that one sacrifice and receive the gift of salvation. Thank you for this priceless gift.

It is by God's will that we have been sanctified through the offering of the body of Jesus Christ once for all. Heb 10:10

Christ's Sacrifice Once for All

HEBREWS 10:1–18 *¹Since the law has only a shadow of the good things to come and not the true form of these realities, it can never, by the same sacrifices that are continually offered year after year, make perfect those who approach. ²Otherwise, would they not have ceased being offered, since the worshipers, cleansed once for all, would no longer have any consciousness of sin? ³But in these sacrifices there is a reminder of sin year after year. ⁴For it is impossible for the blood of bulls and goats to take away sins. ⁵Consequently, when Christ came into the world, he said,*

"Sacrifices and offerings you have not desired,
but a body you have prepared for me;
⁶in burnt offerings and sin offerings
you have taken no pleasure.
⁷Then I said, 'See, God, I have come to do your will, O God'
(in the scroll of the book it is written of me)."

⁸When he said above, "You have neither desired nor taken pleasure in sacrifices and offerings and burnt offerings and sin offerings" (these are offered according to the law), ⁹then he added, "See, I have come to do your will." He abolishes the first in order to establish the second. ¹⁰And it is by God's will that we have been sanctified through the offering of the body of Jesus Christ once for all.

¹¹And every priest stands day after day at his service, offering again and again the same sacrifices that can never take away sins. ¹²But when Christ had offered for all time a single sacrifice for sins, "he sat down at the right hand of God," ¹³and since then has been waiting "until his enemies would be made a footstool for his feet." ¹⁴For by a single offering he has perfected for all time those who are sanctified. ¹⁵And the Holy Spirit also testifies to us, for after saying,

> *¹⁶"This is the covenant that I will make with them*
>   *after those days, says the Lord:*
> *I will put my laws in their hearts,*
>   *and I will write them on their minds,"*

¹⁷he also adds,

> *"I will remember their sins and their lawless deeds no more."*

¹⁸Where there is forgiveness of these, there is no longer any offering for sin.

The sacrifices of the old covenant were only a "shadow" of the good things to come in Christ, not a "true form" of these realities (verse 1). The Old Testament sacrifices were a shadow of the sacrifice of Christ. The Israelites had an indirect relationship to Christ through the shadow. We, however, have a direct relationship through the true form of Christ that has now been revealed. The ancient sacrifices were incomplete and repetitious, whereas the once and for all sacrifice of Christ is perfectly complete.

The sacrifices of the Mosaic law brought a ritual and superficial cleansing of sin, but they were never able to bring about the kind of forgiveness that would bring people inner peace. They were unable to inwardly heal the human conscience from guilt. In fact, these sacrifices were repeated reminders of sin that continually emphasized human guilt and unworthiness before God (verses 2-4).

The new covenant offers us a way to receive authentic forgiveness of sins: "through the offering of the body of Jesus Christ" (verse 10). The author places the words of Psalm 40 on the lips of Jesus (verses 5-9). The obedient will of Jesus, who offered his body and shed his blood, replaces the numerous sacrifices of old. Because of who Christ is and the nature of his self-offering, he offers us complete forgiveness, which is interior, absolving our consciences of guilt. In Christ, we need not try to make up for our sins by our own deeds. Instead, Christ has taken up all our sins and guilt as well as their death-dealing consequences, and offers us true and lasting forgiveness.

The author holds up two images for our reflection. The first is of the many priests standing in the temple, offering sacrifices each day, desperately trying to bring about forgiveness of sins for those who come to worship (verse 11). The second is of one priest, who made one perfect offering for sins, and is now seated at the place of authority with God (verse 12). The priests of the temple are standing, a sign of repeated action that can never be completed; Christ is seated, having accomplished his work. Having won the victory, Christ is now waiting for the results (verse 13). He waits for all his enemies to be made his footstool: injustice, hatred, despair, loneliness, sickness, and death. Between Christ's sacrifice on the cross and his return in glory, we are being perfected and sanctified (verse 14).

The sacrifice of the new covenant is "the offering of the body of Jesus Christ once for all" (verse 10). Yet through the church's eucharistic assembly, the one eternal sacrifice of Christ is re-presented on altars throughout the world until he comes again. The memorial of his ageless sacrifice transcends space and time, making us participants in his own offering at the throne of the Father. The body and blood of Jesus, offered for our sanctification and received in Eucharist, perfects us and invites us to experience God's merciful forgiveness.

Reflection and discussion

• Do I allow myself to experience the complete forgiveness that God wants to give me through the sacrifice of Christ's body and blood?

• What was the positive function of the ancient law of animal sacrifice? Why does the offering of Christ replace the practice of our Israelite ancestors?

• In what ways is the sacrifice of Christ already complete? In what ways are the effects of his sacrifice not yet fully manifested in the world?

• How can I experience Christ's one eternal sacrifice by sharing in the Eucharist?

Prayer

Lord Jesus Christ, by the will of the Father and the work of the Holy Spirit, your death brought life to the world. Through your holy body and blood free me from all sin and evil, help me to trust in your promises, and keep me faithful to you.

SUGGESTIONS FOR FACILITATORS, GROUP SESSION 3

1. Welcome group members and ask if there are any announcements anyone would like to make.

2. You may want to pray this prayer as a group:

God ever faithful, through your ancient covenant you offered your people shadows of the full reality to come. Through prophets and sages you promised your people nourishment, strength, and healing to relieve their deepest hungers and thirsts. Through temple rituals and ancient sacrifices you comforted their fears and anxieties and prepared them for the one eternal sacrifice of the new and everlasting covenant. Through the holy body and blood of Christ your Son, satisfy our hungers, help us experience your forgiveness, and keep us united in the hope of life that lasts forever.

3. Ask one or more of the following questions:
   - What new insight into the mystery of the Eucharist did you gain this week?
   - What encouragement do you need to continue on the path of Bible reading?

4. Discuss lessons 7 through 12. Choose one or more of the questions for reflection and discussion from each lesson to talk over as a group. You may want to ask group members which question was most challenging or helpful to them as you review each lesson.

5. Keep the discussion moving, but don't rush it in order to complete more questions. Allow time for the questions that provoke the most discussion.

6. After talking about each lesson, instruct group members to complete lessons 13 through 18 on their own during the six days before the next group meeting. They should write out their own answers to the questions as preparation for next week's discussion.

7. Ask the group if anyone is having any particular problems with his or her Bible study during the week. You may want to share advice and encouragement within the group.

8. Conclude by praying aloud together the prayer at the end of one of the lessons discussed. You may add to the prayer based on the sharing that has occurred in the group.

**The cup of blessing that we bless, is it not a sharing in the blood of Christ?
The bread that we break, is it not a sharing in the body of Christ?**

1 Cor 10:16

Sharing in the Body and Blood of Christ

1 CORINTHIANS 10:1–22 *¹I do not want you to be unaware, brothers and sisters, that our ancestors were all under the cloud, and all passed through the sea, ²and all were baptized into Moses in the cloud and in the sea, ³and all ate the same spiritual food, ⁴and all drank the same spiritual drink. For they drank from the spiritual rock that followed them, and the rock was Christ. ⁵Nevertheless, God was not pleased with most of them, and they were struck down in the wilderness.*

⁶Now these things occurred as examples for us, so that we might not desire evil as they did. ⁷Do not become idolaters as some of them did; as it is written, "The people sat down to eat and drink, and they rose up to play." ⁸We must not indulge in sexual immorality as some of them did, and twenty-three thousand fell in a single day. ⁹We must not put Christ to the test, as some of them did, and were destroyed by serpents. ¹⁰And do not complain as some of them did, and were destroyed by the destroyer. ¹¹These things happened to them to serve as an example, and they were written down to instruct us, on whom the ends of the ages have come. ¹²So if you think you are standing, watch out that you do not fall. ¹³No testing has overtaken you that is not common to everyone. God is faithful, and he will not let you be tested beyond your strength, but with the testing he will also provide the way out so that you may be able to endure it.

¹⁴Therefore, my dear friends, flee from the worship of idols. ¹⁵I speak as to sensible people; judge for yourselves what I say. ¹⁶The cup of blessing that we bless, is it not a sharing in the blood of Christ? The bread that we break, is it not a sharing in the body of Christ? ¹⁷Because there is one bread, we who are many are one body, for we all partake of the one bread. ¹⁸Consider the people of Israel; are not those who eat the sacrifices partners in the altar? ¹⁹What do I imply then? That food sacrificed to idols is anything, or that an idol is anything? ²⁰No, I imply that what pagans sacrifice, they sacrifice to demons and not to God. I do not want you to be partners with demons. ²¹You cannot drink the cup of the Lord and the cup of demons. You cannot partake of the table of the Lord and the table of demons. ²²Or are we provoking the Lord to jealousy? Are we stronger than he?

The letters of Paul put us into direct contact with the apostolic church and show us that the Eucharist had a central place in the life of the early Christians. Since his letters were to be read in the liturgical assembly, he wrote them imagining himself personally addressing the eucharistic gathering. He frequently adapted greetings, prayers, blessings, and hymns from the Christian liturgy to include in his letters, so that they all express the flavor of the early celebrations of Eucharist. In this passage written to the Corinthians, he provided the early church with important pastoral terminology, describing the Eucharist as "spiritual food" and "spiritual drink" (verse 3), "the cup of blessing that we bless" and "the bread that we break," "sharing in the blood of Christ" and "sharing in the body of Christ" (verse 16), "the cup of the Lord," and "the table of the Lord" (verse 21).

Paul connects the story of the Exodus to the Christian sacraments of baptism and Eucharist. He demonstrates that "our ancestors" were all "baptized into Moses" by standing under the cloud and passing through the sea (verses 1-2). This is a shadow of the spirit and water through which Christians are baptized into Christ. The ancestors also ate "spiritual food" and drank "spiritual drink" in the desert, foreshadowing the full reality to be later shared in the Christian Eucharist (verse 3-4). Paul goes on to show that although the ancestors had received great blessings from God, they still acted in ways that displeased God and they suffered the consequences of their unfaithful choices. Through these examples (verse 11), Paul teaches the Corinthians not to assume God's favor because they have been given the marvelous spiritual nourishment of Christ's presence in the Eucharist. Receiving Christ in the eucharistic assembly requires faithfulness to him and holiness of life.

The immediate problem addressed by Paul was Christians partaking in pagan sacrificial meals offered to idols. Paul explains his prohibition of idol worship by referring to the true communion with Christ experienced by Christians in Eucharist. The union experienced with Christ in Eucharist is real: the cup we bless is a "sharing in the blood of Christ"; the bread we bread is a "sharing in the body of Christ" (verse 16). This communion with Christ also establishes a real unity with other believers who share the Eucharist. Those who partake of the "one bread" become "one body" (verse 17).

God demanded the exclusive allegiance of his people in the desert as he gave them spiritual food and drink; God demands even greater fidelity from those who feed on the body and blood of Christ and become one body in him. Paul agrees that idols are not real, but the demonic powers involved in worshipping any other being besides God are very real. Thus Paul teaches: "You cannot drink the cup of the Lord and the cup of demons. You cannot partake of the table of the Lord and the table of demons" (verse 21). The intimate union we share with Christ in Eucharist demands loyalty and the exclusive devotion of covenant.

Reflection and discussion

• How does Paul use the blessings of Israel in the desert as an example to encourage fidelity to Christ among the people in Corinth?

• In what ways do I experience unity in the body of Christ with other believers when I share the Eucharist? What could I do to create deeper unity among my fellow believers within the church?

• Why does Paul so strongly oppose Christians participating in sacrificial banquets in pagan temples?

• What aspect of the Eucharist does this passage cause me to think about more deeply?

Prayer

Jesus Christ, the spiritual food and drink of our ancestors in the desert prepared us for the true food and drink that is your life with us. Unite us as your church as we eat your body and drink your blood. Keep us faithful to you in uncompromising devotion.

**For as often as you eat this bread and drink the cup,
you proclaim the Lord's death until he comes.** 1 Cor 11:26

Remembering the Lord Until He Comes

1 CORINTHIANS 11:17–29 *¹⁷Now in the following instructions I do not commend you, because when you come together it is not for the better but for the worse. ¹⁸For, to begin with, when you come together as a church, I hear that there are divisions among you; and to some extent I believe it. ¹⁹Indeed, there have to be factions among you, for only so will it become clear who among you are genuine. ²⁰When you come together, it is not really to eat the Lord's supper. ²¹For when the time comes to eat, each of you goes ahead with your own supper, and one goes hungry and another becomes drunk. ²²What! Do you not have homes to eat and drink in? Or do you show contempt for the church of God and humiliate those who have nothing? What should I say to you? Should I commend you? In this matter I do not commend you!*

²³For I received from the Lord what I also handed on to you, that the Lord Jesus on the night when he was betrayed took a loaf of bread, ²⁴and when he had given thanks, he broke it and said, "This is my body that is for you. Do this in remembrance of me." ²⁵In the same way he took the cup also, after supper, saying, "This cup is the new covenant in my blood. Do this, as often as you drink it, in remembrance of me." ²⁶For as often as you eat this bread and drink the cup, you proclaim the Lord's death until he comes.

²⁷Whoever, therefore, eats the bread or drinks the cup of the Lord in an unwor-

thy manner will be answerable for the body and blood of the Lord. [28] *Examine your-selves, and only then eat of the bread and drink of the cup.* [29] *For all who eat and drink without discerning the body, eat and drink judgment against themselves.*

Tradition, the faithful handing on of what was received, forms the church's identity. The eucharistic tradition of Christ's Last Supper has come down to us in four different forms: three in the gospel narratives and one here in Paul's letter (verses 23-25). Each of the four formula show discreet variations, representing adaptations to the unique settings of each community and the hand of different New Testament authors, yet each is a faithful handing on of what Jesus himself gave to his church. Paul presents himself as a link in the chain of eucharistic tradition: "I received from the Lord what I also handed on to you" (verse 23). Paul challenges the church in Corinth to be faithful to what he handed on to them and what they received. The community had to make the words and actions of Christ their own, to faithfully carry on the tradition as a vital element of their commitment to be with their Lord.

The Eucharist in the early church continued to be celebrated, like the Last Supper, in the context of a meal. The assemblies consisted of rich and poor, slaves and free persons, women and men, all meeting together in the larger homes of the communities. But this most central and defining celebration became plagued with problems in Corinth. Divisions and factions developed (verse 18). Some went hungry while others indulged (verse 21). The poor were humiliated because they had nothing to eat (verse 22). Paul was horrified that social hierarchies and economic factions had infiltrated the church's central act of worship. The assembly was not even worthy to be called "the Lord's Supper" (verse 20).The words and gestures given by Christ to his church had become empty because the community was no longer doing what Jesus did, giving his life in self-emptying love. The Eucharist was to be a meal of generous self-giving, a communion in which people formerly divided by race, class, and gender became one body in Christ.

Paul reminds the community of the words and actions of Jesus at the Last Supper in order to correct their understanding and practice of the Eucharist. Jesus pronounced that the broken bread is "my body that is for you" and that the cup is "the new covenant in my blood" (verses 24-25). Christ' redemptive death for others and his inauguration of the new covenant is the central meaning of the Eucharist. The Corinthians must learn to celebrate the Lord's Supper in a way that demonstrates how profoundly the Lord's death has changed the condition of people's relationships with one another and the responsibilities of people bound with God in covenant obligations.

Paul then adds his own understanding of the meaning of Eucharist: "For as often as you eat this bread and drink the cup, you proclaim the Lord's death until he comes" (verse 26). The Eucharist asserts the past, the redemptive death of Jesus, the present, the community that experiences salvation in eating and drinking his body and blood, and the future, the glorious coming of Christ. The Eucharist looks backward to the Lord's death and forward to his return, bringing both past and future into the present moment as the community remembers his dying and anticipates his coming.

Sharing the Eucharist "in an unworthy manner" (verse 27), in this context, means eating and drinking in a way that causes division, shows disregard for the poor and hungry, and forgets the obligations of the covenant. Self-centeredness, individualism, and arrogance make one "answerable for the body and blood of the Lord," that is, responsible for his death and guilty of dishonoring the Eucharist. So Christians who are preparing to share communion in Christ must "examine" themselves to make sure they are in a fit state to partake in the holy supper (verse 28). Those who eat and drink at the Eucharist "without discerning the body" eat and drink their own judgment (verse 29). Worthy communion means realizing the presence of the living Christ and the corporate unity of all who share his life.

Reflection and discussion

• Why does Paul remind the Corinthians of the eucharistic tradition that has been handed on to them?

• In what way does the Eucharist bring the past and the future into one timeless moment?

• What is the best way for me to examine myself in order to prepare to celebrate Eucharist with the community of faith?

• In what ways is my church like the church in Corinth as it celebrates Eucharist? How do the words of Paul challenge me to change?

Prayer

Living Lord, you have handed on the Eucharist to your church through the apostles, and you call us to proclaim your saving death until you return in glory. Help me to examine myself and prepare for the eucharistic liturgy so that I will reflect your self-giving love for all people.

Taking the five loaves and the two fish, he looked up to heaven,
and blessed and broke the loaves,
and gave them to his disciples to set before the people. Mark 6:41

Feeding the Crowd with Loaves and Fish

MARK 6:30–44 *³⁰The apostles gathered around Jesus, and told him all that they had done and taught. ³¹He said to them, "Come away to a deserted place all by yourselves and rest a while." For many were coming and going, and they had no leisure even to eat. ³²And they went away in the boat to a deserted place by themselves. ³³Now many saw them going and recognized them, and they hurried there on foot from all the towns and arrived ahead of them. ³⁴As he went ashore, he saw a great crowd; and he had compassion for them, because they were like sheep without a shepherd; and he began to teach them many things. ³⁵When it grew late, his disciples came to him and said, "This is a deserted place, and the hour is now very late; ³⁶send them away so that they may go into the surrounding country and villages and buy something for themselves to eat." ³⁷But he answered them, "You give them something to eat." They said to him, "Are we to go and buy two hundred denarii worth of bread, and give it to them to eat?" ³⁸And he said to them, "How many loaves have you? Go and see." When they had found out, they said, "Five, and two fish." ³⁹Then he ordered them to get all the people to sit down in groups on the green grass. ⁴⁰So they sat down in groups of hundreds and of fifties. ⁴¹Taking the five loaves and the two fish, he looked up to heaven, and blessed and broke the loaves, and gave them to his disciples to set* *before the people; and he divided the two fish among them all.* *⁴²And all ate and were filled;* *⁴³and they took up twelve baskets full of broken pieces and of the fish.* *⁴⁴Those who had eaten the loaves numbered five thousand men.*

The account of Jesus feeding the multitude occurs in all four of the gospels, attesting both to its popularity among the early Christians and its importance for the community. Though it is impossible to determine exactly how the crowd was fed, the event clearly made a deep impression on Jesus' followers, beginning with his early disciples and continuing through the ages as the story was expressed in liturgical reading, biblical text, and Christian art. The feeding story excites our imaginations and directs us to contemplate the power of Jesus' presence in our midst.

When interpreted in light of the eucharistic liturgy, the account of Jesus nourishing the vast crowd was seen by the early Christians as a concrete foreshadowing of the Eucharist. In fact, Mark wrote the feeding account as a eucharistic story. Viewing the vast feeding through the lens of the church's eucharistic tradition, Mark showed in his gospel account what the feeding narrative meant for the church in his day. The connections are clear as we notice words and gestures familiar from the Last Supper narratives used to describe Jesus' actions in feeding the crowds. Jesus took the loaves and fish, "looked up to heaven, and blessed and broke the loaves, and gave them to his disciples" (verse 41). In the feeding narrative, the word of blessing has a supernatural power to change and multiply the bread. Listening to the narrative of the feeding account in the liturgy of the Word prepares the listeners to behold another miraculous feeding that will take place in the liturgy of the Eucharist.

The early Christians also looked to the Old Testament to help them express the deeper meaning of the feeding narrative. The account bears a remarkable resemblance to the story of Elisha's multiplication of the loaves in 2 Kings 4:42–44. One hundred men were fed from twenty barley loaves and a few ears of grain. Despite objections that the quantity was inadequate, Elisha distributed the food and insisted that the people would eat, trusting in the word of the Lord: "They shall eat and have some left" (2 Kings 4:43). Trusting in God's word, Jesus feeds his people with abundant food that more than satisfies.

The feeding of the crowd by Jesus in "a deserted place" (verses 31-32, 35) also recalls God's feeding his people in the desert of the Exodus. The bread and the fish echo the manna and the quail by which God provided for the hungry Israelites on their journey through the wilderness. Moses, the prophet of the covenant with Israel, was the instrument of God's feeding in response to the complaining of the people. They had not yet learned where to turn for their source of life and daily bread. Jesus, the mediator of the new covenant, has compassion on the hungry crowd and gives them food in abundance that prepares them for the food that lasts.

Jesus passes on the responsibility for feeding hungry people to his disciples. In response to the disciples' request to "send them away," Jesus tells them, "You give them something to eat" (verses 36-37). God taught the Israelites in the desert to rely on him for their daily nourishment; Jesus taught his disciples to serve the needs of his people. Later in the gospel, Jesus will provide the leaders of the Christian community with a more substantial means of feeding his people in Eucharist.

Reflection and discussion

• How does Mark's gospel demonstrate that the story of Jesus' feeding the crowd is a eucharistic narrative?

• How are the nourishing gifts that Jesus provided to the crowds foreshadowed in the works of Moses and Elisha?

• How does God provide for me in life's wilderness? Do I trust that God will give me what I need for each day?

• Why does Jesus say to his apostles, "You give them something to eat"? What is the message for me?

• What does the narrative of the loaves and fish teach me about the meaning of Eucharist?

Prayer

Lord Jesus, you feed and nourish your people in abundance. Grateful for the many gifts you have given to me, may I heed your appeal, "You give them something to eat." Inspire me to respond to your call to feed our hungry world.

He took the seven loaves, and after giving thanks he broke them and gave them to his disciples to distribute; and they distributed them to the crowd.

Mark 8:6

The One Bread for All People

MARK 8:1–21 ¹*In those days when there was again a great crowd without anything to eat, he called his disciples and said to them,* ²*"I have compassion for the crowd, because they have been with me now for three days and have nothing to eat.* ³*If I send them away hungry to their homes, they will faint on the way— and some of them have come from a great distance."* ⁴*His disciples replied, "How can one feed these people with bread here in the desert?"* ⁵*He asked them, "How many loaves do you have?" They said, "Seven."* ⁶*Then he ordered the crowd to sit down on the ground; and he took the seven loaves, and after giving thanks he broke them and gave them to his disciples to distribute; and they distributed them to the crowd.* ⁷*They had also a few small fish; and after blessing them, he ordered that these too should be distributed.* ⁸*They ate and were filled; and they took up the broken pieces left over, seven baskets full.* ⁹*Now there were about four thousand people. And he sent them away.* ¹⁰*And immediately he got into the boat with his disciples and went to the district of Dalmanutha.*

¹¹*The Pharisees came and began to argue with him, asking him for a sign from heaven, to test him.* ¹²*And he sighed deeply in his spirit and said, "Why does this generation ask for a sign? Truly I tell you, no sign will be given to this generation."* ¹³*And he left them, and getting into the boat again, he went across to the other side.*

¹⁴Now the disciples had forgotten to bring any bread; and they had only one loaf with them in the boat. ¹⁵And he cautioned them, saying, "Watch out—beware of the yeast of the Pharisees and the yeast of Herod." ¹⁶They said to one another, "It is because we have no bread." ¹⁷And becoming aware of it, Jesus said to them, "Why are you talking about having no bread? Do you still not perceive or understand? Are your hearts hardened? ¹⁸Do you have eyes, and fail to see? Do you have ears, and fail to hear? And do you not remember? ¹⁹When I broke the five loaves for the five thousand, how many baskets full of broken pieces did you collect?" They said to him, "Twelve." ²⁰"And the seven for the four thousand, how many baskets full of broken pieces did you collect?" And they said to him, "Seven." ²¹Then he said to them, "Do you not yet understand?"

Mark's decision to devote space to two accounts of the same sort of miracle suggests that each one had a special significance for him and that neither could be omitted without losing something important. The term "bread" (or loaves) appears sixteen times in chapters 6–8, which incorporate the two feeding accounts, and only once in the remainder of the gospel when Jesus declares that the bread is his body (14:22). In the two narratives, the gospel uses eucharistic imagery to express the universal mission that Jesus desires for his church. The first miracle takes place on the side of the Sea of Galilee where Jews reside; the second occurs on the side inhabited by Gentiles. The twin accounts demonstrate that Jesus is the one bread for both Jews and Gentiles, the bread of life for the whole world.

Crossing the sea from the Jewish to the Gentile shore proved extremely difficult. Adverse winds combined with the disciples' resistance, "for they did not understand about the loaves" (6:52), made the journey challenging and perilous. Jesus had to show his disciples the faith of a Gentile woman (7:24–30) and to give hearing and speech to a Gentile man (7:31–37) before his disciples could join with Gentiles as well as Jews in the breaking of the bread. The difficult passage expresses the struggle experienced by the early church in accepting all people into fellowship with Christ and gathering Jews and Gentiles around one common table.

The subtle changes between the two feeding narratives suggests that the first expresses the church's mission to the Jews, while the second feeding symbolizes the mission to the whole world. In this second account, the number fed is four thousand—four representing the four corners of the earth or the four points on a compass. There is also the note that "some of them have come from a great distance" (verse 3), indicating the Gentiles from all over the empire who would eventually join the church. Likewise the number of loaves and the number of baskets of fragments is "seven," a number frequently used in the Bible to represent universal wholeness or completeness. Even the terms the writer uses for "baskets" are different in each account: in the first, the basket is a wicker container used by the Jews to carry food; in the second, the basket is a much larger container found in Gentile settings.

Mark's two stories of feeding the crowds reflect two stages in the development of the Eucharist. The first feeding account is shaped by the church's earlier Jewish setting. Here Jesus not only took, blessed, and broke the five loaves but also the two fish, indicating a stage when the Eucharist was still a full meal. The second account is shaped by a later setting in which Christians of Gentile origin had been integrated into the community. Here the fish are separated from the main action and Jesus takes the seven loaves, gives thanks, and breaks them (verse 6), indicating a period when the Eucharist was no longer a full meal. The fish were mentioned separately as a postscript (verse 7). The action of Jesus over the bread, "giving thanks," is *eucharistesas*, in Greek, the origin of our word Eucharist.

After the feeding account, Jesus again got into the boat with his disciples. When the disciples realized they had not brought a supply of bread with them, the texts notes, "They had only one loaf with them in the boat" (verse 14). The boat is a symbol of Christ's church, and the one loaf is the one bread, Jesus himself, needed by Jews and Gentiles alike. Mark expressed in narrative form what Paul expressed in a statement: "Because there is one bread, we who are many are one body, for we all partake of the one bread" (1 Cor 10:17). The early Christians understood the gathering up of the fragments as a prefiguring of the gathering up of God's people into the fellowship of the church. All people, Jews and Gentiles, men and women, slaves and free persons, all are called to share in the one bread that is Christ and to become his body living in the world.

Reflection and discussion

• Why did Mark include two very similar feeding stories in his gospel? Why did he not choose to omit one of them?

• What are the most significant differences between the two feeding accounts?

• In what ways do the feeding narratives demonstrate that Jesus is the one bread for both Jews and Gentiles?

Prayer

Lord Jesus, you are bread for all the world, nourishing all people who come to satisfy their hungry hearts. May we who eat of the one bread of life become the one body of Christ alive in the world.

**"You do not know what you are asking.
Are you able to drink the cup that I drink?"** Mark 10:38

Drinking from the Cup of Christ

MARK 10:35–45 *35 James and John, the sons of Zebedee, came forward to [Jesus] and said to him, "Teacher, we want you to do for us whatever we ask of you." 36 And he said to them, "What is it you want me to do for you?" 37 And they said to him, "Grant us to sit, one at your right hand and one at your left, in your glory." 38 But Jesus said to them, "You do not know what you are asking. Are you able to drink the cup that I drink, or be baptized with the baptism that I am baptized with?" 39 They replied, "We are able." Then Jesus said to them, "The cup that I drink you will drink; and with the baptism with which I am baptized, you will be baptized; 40 but to sit at my right hand or at my left is not mine to grant, but it is for those for whom it has been prepared."*

41 When the ten heard this, they began to be angry with James and John. 42 So Jesus called them and said to them, "You know that among the Gentiles those whom they recognize as their rulers lord it over them, and their great ones are tyrants over them. 43 But it is not so among you; but whoever wishes to become great among you must be your servant, 44 and whoever wishes to be first among you must be slave of all. 45 For the Son of Man came not to be served but to serve, and to give his life a ransom for many."

MARK 14:32–36

[superscript 32] *They went to a place called Gethsemane; and he said to his disciples, "Sit here while I pray."* [superscript 33] *He took with him Peter and James and John, and began to be distressed and agitated.* [superscript 34] *And said to them, "I am deeply grieved, even to death; remain here, and keep awake."* [superscript 35] *And going a little farther, he threw himself on the ground and prayed that, if it were possible, the hour might pass from him.* [superscript 36] *He said, "Abba, Father, for you all things are possible; remove this cup from me; yet, not what I want, but what you want."*

Following the episodes that focus on Jesus as the one bread for all people, the gospel narrative turns more explicitly toward Christ's passion. Jesus gives a series of three passion predictions (8:31–38; 9:30–37; 10:32–45) in which he foretells his approaching suffering, death, and resurrection, suggesting the implications of his passion for Christian discipleship. While the actions of breaking and eating the plentiful bread highlight the first half of the gospel, joining in Christ's death by drinking his cup is emphasized in the remainder. With the symbol of bread, the gospel concentrates on the disciples' responsibility to feed all God's people with the nourishment that is Christ. With the symbol of the cup, the gospel focuses on the commitment necessary to care for God's people by sharing in Christ's suffering.

After the third passion prediction of Jesus, as Jesus and his disciples made their fateful turn up the road to Jerusalem, James and John asked that they sit at the left and right of Jesus in the glory of his kingdom. With their eyes only on the splendor they imagine for themselves, Jesus offers them a lesson in servant-leadership. He introduced the image of the cup and asked if they were willing and able to drink it: "Are you able to drink the cup that I drink, or be baptized with the baptism that I am baptized with?" (10:38). They said they could and Jesus said they will: "The cup that I drink you will drink; and with the baptism with which I am baptized, you will be baptized" (verse 39).

In the Old Testament, the "cup" expresses God's blessings, as in Psalm 23 where the psalmist proclaims, "my cup overflows" (Ps 23:5); or more often the cup expresses God' wrath and judgment against sin. In Psalm 116:13, "the cup of salvation" is a libation, an offering of wine to God, spilled out as a sacrifice on the temple's altar. All of these understandings of the cup enrich the New Testament understanding of drinking the cup. Jesus' pledge that his disciples would drink the cup that he drinks is an assurance that they would share in his cross through trials and suffering of their own. Drinking the cup, identifying with the passion and death of Jesus, means not only being willing to suffer, but offering one's own life in union with Christ to the Father.

The final reference to the cup is found in Jesus' prayer in Gethsemane as he anticipates his betrayal and passion. Even Jesus, who had invited his disciples to drink the cup of redemptive suffering with him, recoils from the challenge. Praying to his Father, he pleads, "Remove this cup from me; yet, not what I want, but what you want" (14:36). His anguish grows as he experiences the full weight of the Father's judgment against sin fall on himself. He chooses to drink the cup and experience his passion in order "to give his life a ransom for many" (10:45), so that sinners may be redeemed. The cup of God's wrath becomes, in Christ, the cup of salvation and blessing.

Reflection and discussion

• Why does Mark emphasize the sharing of bread in the first half of his gospel and drinking from the cup in the second half?

• How does the "cup of salvation" (Ps 116:13) prefigure the eucharistic cup of Christ's blood? What does the symbolism of drinking the cup teach me about the full implications of sharing in the cup of the Eucharist?

Prayer

Suffering Redeemer, you have made your cup of suffering into a cup of blessing and salvation for us. Give me the courage and the love to drink from the cup of which you drink, and help me to understand more fully the commitment I make when I drink from the cup of Eucharist.

While they were eating, he took a loaf of bread, and after blessing it he broke it, gave it to them, and said, "Take; this is my body." Mark 14:22

The Meal of the New Passover

MARK 14:12–26 *¹²On the first day of Unleavened Bread, when the Passover lamb is sacrificed, his disciples said to him, "Where do you want us to go and make the preparations for you to eat the Passover?" ¹³So he sent two of his disciples, saying to them, "Go into the city, and a man carrying a jar of water will meet you; follow him, ¹⁴and wherever he enters, say to the owner of the house, 'The Teacher asks, Where is my guest room where I may eat the Passover with my disciples?' ¹⁵He will show you a large room upstairs, furnished and ready. Make preparations for us there." ¹⁶So the disciples set out and went to the city, and found everything as he had told them; and they prepared the Passover meal.*

¹⁷When it was evening, he came with the twelve. ¹⁸And when they had taken their places and were eating, Jesus said, "Truly I tell you, one of you will betray me, one who is eating with me." ¹⁹They began to be distressed and to say to him one after another, "Surely, not I?" ²⁰He said to them, "It is one of the twelve, one who is dipping bread into the bowl with me. ²¹For the Son of Man goes as it is written of him, but woe to that one by whom the Son of Man is betrayed! It would have been better for that one not to have been born."

²²While they were eating, he took a loaf of bread, and after blessing it he broke it, gave it to them, and said, "Take; this is my body." ²³Then he took a cup, and after giving thanks he gave it to them, and all of them drank from it. ²⁴He said to

them, "This is my blood of the covenant, which is poured out for many. ²⁵ Truly I
tell you, I will never again drink of the fruit of the vine until that day when I
drink it new in the kingdom of God."

²⁶ *When they had sung the hymn, they went out to the Mount of Olives.*

Mark, Matthew, and Luke place the Last Supper on the eve of Passover and so present it as a Passover meal. The Last Supper is also connected with the feast of Unleavened Bread, a festival remembering the departure of the Israelites from Egypt. As the Passover meal personally connects each new generation of Jews to the liberation from slavery in Egypt, the Eucharist connects followers of Jesus with his liberating victory over sin and death. Jesus transformed the ancient Passover supper into the sacrament whereby people of all times may enter into the redemption won for us by Jesus on the cross.

The Last Supper takes place within a context of both solidarity and betrayal. The disciples demonstrate their unity in the traditions of Israel and their bond with Jesus in the preparations for the Passover meal. Yet, the supper takes place amidst betrayal, plotting, and denial. Jesus contrasts the heinous betrayal of Judas with the intimacy of the meal: "It is one of the twelve, one who is dipping bread into the bowl with me" (verses 18-20). The bond that Jesus creates with his disciples through his words and actions at the meal are even more striking in this setting. Disciples of all times must ask themselves in the midst of the church's Eucharist, "Surely, not I?"

The institution of the Eucharist (verses 22-24) presents Jesus not as the passive victim of a tragic crime, but the active hero who gives his life for others. The words and actions of Jesus over the bread and wine transform the Last Supper from the final meal of a doomed prisoner to a sacrament of self-giving and generous love. The dying Servant gave his own body and blood, his very self, so that all might live.

When describing Jesus' offer of the cup to his disciples, Mark adds his own unique words, "All of them drank from it" (verse 23). When James and John had agreed to drink the cup (10:38–39), they did not realize what they were saying. Those who follow Jesus must be willing to enter into his generous self-offering for others. With the cup Jesus offers to all of his disciples an intimate solidarity with him and a participation in his redemptive passion and death.

The words "blood of the covenant" (verse 24) are a clear excerpt from the covenant at Sinai, when Moses splattered the blood of the sacrifice on the altar and on the people (Exod 24:5–8). The blood expressed the sharing of all the people in the life of the victim, and the sacrificed lamb ratified the bond between God and his people. But Jesus gives his very self, his body and blood, as the complete covenant sacrifice. The animal of the ancient covenant was neither divine nor human, but now the covenant is ratified in the blood of Jesus, who is both human and divine. He is the perfect sacrifice "poured out for many," so that all who drink the cup will be redeemed from the bondage of sin and death.

In the midst of the betrayal and suffering of the Last Supper, there is heroic self-giving and hope for the future. The final words of Jesus, "I will never again drink of the fruit of the vine until that day when I drink it new in the kingdom of God" (verse 25), makes the Last Supper and every subsequent Eucharist an anticipation of the future joys of the kingdom. Every Eucharist throughout the ages is a timeless offering, holding together the past, present, and future: the sacrificial death of Jesus, the covenant in his body and blood, and the coming of the kingdom.

Reflection and discussion

• Why did the gospel writers associate the Last Supper with the Passover meal of Israel? How does Jesus transform the bread and wine of the Passover meal?

• How does Jesus transform his last, tragic meal into an everlasting sacrament of love?

• In what way do both Paul (1 Cor 11:26) and Mark include the past and future in the Christian Eucharist?

• How is Christ the ideal covenant sacrifice? What is my commitment when I drink the cup of his blood?

Prayer

Suffering Servant, at the Last Supper you give your church the Eucharist as the everlasting sacrament of your body and blood. As I eat your body and drink your blood, free me from the bondage of sin and death and join me in intimate covenant with you and with your disciples.

SUGGESTIONS FOR FACILITATORS, GROUP SESSION 4

1. Welcome group members and ask if anyone has any questions, announcements, or requests.

2. You may want to pray this prayer as a group:

Lord Jesus, you are the one bread for all people and the cup of salvation that brings redemption to all who share in your life. As we read the texts of the New Testament, you show us the richness of Eucharist as the food that nourishes our deepest needs, the blood of the everlasting covenant, the Passover meal that gives us true freedom, the sacrifice of your passion and death, and the foretaste of the banquet in your kingdom. As we eat your body and drink your blood, may we proclaim your death until you come in glory.

3. Ask one or more of the following questions:

- What is the most difficult part of this study for you?

- What did you learn anew about the Eucharist this week?

4. Discuss lessons 13 through 18. Choose one or more of the questions for reflection and discussion from each lesson to discuss as a group. You may want to ask group members which question was most challenging or helpful to them as you review each lesson.

5. Keep the discussion moving, but allow time for the questions that provoke the most discussion. Encourage the group members to use "I" language in their responses.

6. After talking over each lesson, instruct group members to complete lessons 19 through 24 on their own during the six days before the next group meeting. They should write out their own answers to the questions as preparation for next week's session.

7. Conclude by praying aloud together the prayer at the end of one of the lessons discussed. You may choose to conclude the prayer by asking members to pray aloud any requests they may have.

Give us this day our daily bread. And forgive us our debts, as we also have forgiven our debtors. Matt 6:11–12

Praying to Our Father

MATTHEW 6:7–15

[7]*"When you are praying, do not heap up empty phrases as the Gentiles do; for they think that they will be heard because of their many words.* [8]*Do not be like them, for your Father knows what you need before you ask him.*

[9]*Pray then in this way:*
Our Father in heaven,
hallowed be your name.
[10]*Your kingdom come.*
Your will be done,
*   on earth as it is in heaven.*
[11]*Give us this day our daily bread.*
[12]*And forgive us our debts,*
*   as we also have forgiven our debtors.*
[13]*And do not bring us to the time of trial,*
*   but rescue us from the evil one.*
[14]*For if you forgive others their trespasses, your heavenly Father will also forgive you;* [15]*but if you do not forgive others, neither will your Father forgive your trespasses."*

The Our Father is the prayer of Jesus, the prayer that he taught his disciples when they asked him how to pray. It has been called the prayer par excellence because when we pray it with Jesus, our voices blend with his and our hearts open to our Father in heaven. It can be prayed by an individual or by a community, but it is always a prayer in union with the church. For this reason it has a special place at the church's worship and has long been a prominent part of the eucharistic ritual. When the church gathers around the table of the Lord in Eucharist, it most fully expresses humanity in prayer before God.

When Jesus taught his disciples to pray, he did much more than give them a simple prayer they could memorize and repeat. Jesus showed them how to address God with intimacy and trust. The prayer that Jesus taught us is directed to the Father, as was Jesus' whole life of dedicated offering. He taught us to pray to "our Father" (verse 9) because we offer up our prayers, works, joys, and sufferings through Christ, in Christ, and with Christ, in the unity of the Spirit, to our Father. When we make the Our Father our own at the eucharistic liturgy, we are personally united to the saving action of Christ that is taking place in the church's worship.

The Our Father is a prayer that is oriented toward the future. It exhorts us to pray for the coming of the kingdom even as we celebrate the Lord's presence in our midst (verse 10). When prayed in eucharistic worship, the Our Father expresses our joyful longing for that time in which there will be no more sadness and pain, when sin and death have vanished, when salvation will be manifested in every corner of the globe and in every corner of our hearts. We pray with Jesus for the full realization, "on earth as it is in heaven," of that prayer he offered in Gethsemane immediately after the Last Supper: "your will be done."

One of the ways the early Christians referred to the Eucharist was "our *epiousios* bread," which we usually translate in the Our Father as "our daily bread." The meaning of the Greek adjective is uncertain because it is found nowhere else in ancient Greek literature. Literally it means "super-essential," and it was translated by St. Jerome as "supersubstantial." Many biblical commentators suggest that the early Christians coined this new word to refer to their new experience of Eucharist, a unique meal like no other in which the Risen Lord was present to his followers. Though the kingdom is coming in the future, we have a foretaste of that banquet today in "our bread, "our meal," the bread of life.

Reflection and discussion

• What makes prayer sincere and genuine? Why is the Our Father such an ideal prayer?

• Why is the Our Father always prayed when gathering at the Lord's table for communion?

• What verses of the Our Father do I want to focus on today?

Prayer

Our Father, hallowed be your name. May we long for the coming of your kingdom as we celebrate the presence of your Son among us. Forgive our sins as we forgive one another. Give us today the bread that sustains us forever.

"Drink from it, all of you; for this is my blood of the covenant,
which is poured out for many for the forgiveness of sins." Matt 26:27–28

The Blood of the Covenant Poured Out

MATTHEW 26:17–29 *¹⁷On the first day of Unleavened Bread the disciples came to Jesus, saying, "Where do you want us to make the preparations for you to eat the Passover?" ¹⁸He said, "Go into the city to a certain man, and say to him, 'The Teacher says, My time is near; I will keep the Passover at your house with my disciples.'" ¹⁹So the disciples did as Jesus had directed them, and they prepared the Passover meal.*

²⁰When it was evening, he took his place with the twelve; ²¹and while they were eating, he said, "Truly I tell you, one of you will betray me." ²²And they became greatly distressed and began to say to him one after another, "Surely not I, Lord?" ²³He answered, "The one who has dipped his hand into the bowl with me will betray me. ²⁴The Son of Man goes as it is written of him, but woe to that one by whom the Son of Man is betrayed! It would have been better for that one not to have been born." ²⁵Judas, who betrayed him, said, "Surely not I, Rabbi?" He replied, "You have said so."

²⁶While they were eating, Jesus took a loaf of bread, and after blessing it he broke it, gave it to the disciples, and said, "Take, eat; this is my body." ²⁷Then he took a cup, and after giving thanks he gave it to them, saying, "Drink from it, all of you; ²⁸for this is my blood of the covenant, which is poured out for many for the forgiveness of sins. ²⁹I tell you, I will never again drink of this fruit of the vine until that day when I drink it new with you in my Father's kingdom."

The account of the Last Supper in Matthew's gospel is very similar to that in Mark's gospel. Jesus identifies the broken bread of the Passover meal with his own body and the cup with his own blood poured out. Yet Matthew heightens the sacrificial nature of the supper by adding the words "for the forgiveness of sins" (verse 28). For Matthew, the forgiveness of sins is a primary purpose of Christ's death and of the sacramental offering of his blood in the Eucharist. In drinking the eucharistic cup, his disciples participate in his "blood of the covenant." By uniting themselves with Christ's sacrificial forgiveness of others, their own sins are forgiven.

Matthew prepared his readers throughout his gospel to understand Christ's sacrifice for the forgiveness of sins. In the Sermon on the Mount, Jesus taught his disciples to pray: "And forgive us our debts, as we also have forgiven our debtors" (6:12). Then he chose this phrase of the prayer for further commentary: "For if you forgive others their trespasses, your heavenly Father will also forgive you; but if you do not forgive others, neither will your Father forgive your trespasses" (6:14–15). Jesus continues to teach about forgiveness later in Matthew's gospel in his discourse on relationships within the church. When Peter asks Jesus how often he should forgive a brother or sister, Jesus suggests that forgiveness should not be measured (18:22). It is in this spirit of forgiveness of one another that disciples of Jesus should celebrate Eucharist "for the forgiveness of sins."

The eucharistic cup recalls the blood of the ancient covenant. In giving instructions to Moses for sacrifices, God declared that blood is sacred: "I have given it to you for making atonement for your lives on the altar; for, as life, it is the blood that makes atonement" (Lev 17:11). The blood of the animal victim was offered to God in atonement for the sins of humans. The sacrifice of Jesus, however, was quite different from the sacrifices of old. His sacrifice on the cross, sacramentally made present in the Eucharist, was a personal act of mercy. Twice in Matthew's gospel, Jesus quotes the words of God through the prophet Hosea: "I desire mercy, not sacrifice" (9:13; 12:7; Hos 6:6). God desires a personal response, not just the offering of animal victims. Jesus showed mercy to sinners through shedding his blood and offering them forgiveness of their sins.

The covenant confirmed by the blood of Christ is the "new covenant" spoken of by Jeremiah. In foretelling this new covenant written on the hearts of God's people (Jer 31:33), Jeremiah spoke the word of the Lord: "For I will forgive their iniquity and remember their sin no more" (Jer 31:34). The new covenant was based on God's mercy and forgiveness, sealed in the blood of Christ "poured out for many for the forgiveness of sins" (verse 28). Jesus himself is the Suffering Servant foretold by the prophet Isaiah. He was "wounded for our transgressions, crushed for our iniquities," and "the Lord has laid upon him the iniquity of us all" (Isa 53:5–6). As Jesus accepted for himself the cup of suffering and death, he passed on to us the cup of forgiveness and life.

Reflection and discussion

• In what way does Matthew emphasize the sacrificial aspects of the Eucharist?

• Is God's forgiveness of us automatic when we celebrate the Eucharist, or is something else required of us? What does this challenge me to do before receiving the Eucharist?

• Why does God desire mercy and not sacrifice? How does the self-offering of Jesus fulfill God's desire?

Prayer

Lord Jesus, you gave us the Eucharist as your broken body and your blood poured out. Thank you for the forgiveness of sins you offer to the world in this sacrifice. Help me to show mercy and forgiveness to others so that I might receive forgiveness in your Eucharist.

"When you give a banquet, invite the poor, the crippled, the lame, and the blind. And you will be blessed, because they cannot repay you, for you will be repaid at the resurrection of the righteous." Luke 14:13–14

Parable of the Great Banquet

LUKE 14:7–24 *⁷When he noticed how the guests chose the places of honor, he told them a parable. ⁸"When you are invited by someone to a wedding banquet, do not sit down at the place of honor, in case someone more distinguished than you has been invited by your host; ⁹and the host who invited both of you may come and say to you, 'Give this person your place,' and then in disgrace you would start to take the lowest place. ¹⁰But when you are invited, go and sit down at the lowest place, so that when your host comes, he may say to you, 'Friend, move up higher'; then you will be honored in the presence of all who sit at the table with you. ¹¹For all who exalt themselves will be humbled, and those who humble themselves will be exalted."*

¹²He said also to the one who had invited him, "When you give a luncheon or a dinner, do not invite your friends or your brothers or your relatives or rich neighbors, in case they may invite you in return, and you would be repaid. ¹³But when you give a banquet, invite the poor, the crippled, the lame, and the blind. ¹⁴And you will be blessed, because they cannot repay you, for you will be repaid at the resurrection of the righteous."

¹⁵One of the dinner guests, on hearing this, said to him, "Blessed is anyone who will eat bread in the kingdom of God!" ¹⁶Then Jesus said to him, "Someone gave a great dinner and invited many. [17]*At the time for the dinner he sent his slave to say to those who had been invited, 'Come; for everything is ready now.'* [18]*But they all alike began to make excuses. The first said to him, 'I have bought a piece of land, and I must go out and see it; please accept my regrets.'* [19]*Another said, 'I have bought five yoke of oxen, and I am going to try them out; please accept my regrets.'* [20]*Another said, 'I have just been married, and therefore I cannot come.'* [21]*So the slave returned and reported this to his master. Then the owner of the house became angry and said to his slave, 'Go out at once into the streets and lanes of the town and bring in the poor, the crippled, the blind, and the lame.'* [22]*And the slave said, 'Sir, what you ordered has been done, and there is still room.'* [23]*Then the master said to the slave, 'Go out into the roads and lanes, and compel people to come in, so that my house may be filled.* [24]*For I tell you, none of those who were invited will taste my dinner.'"*

Throughout the gospel of Luke, meals and parables about meals express the teachings that Jesus wants to offer his church about the Eucharist and its completion in the banquet of God's kingdom. In a series of ten meals throughout the gospel, Luke presents the qualities of the church's Eucharist and the relationship of the Eucharist to the church's ministry and mission. The banquet images of Isaiah form the imagery of Jesus' teachings. The feast of wine, bread, and rich food is not limited to those with sufficient means or social standing. The only requirement is a genuine hunger and thirst. People will come from many nations to share in the abundant life of the anticipated messianic banquet (Isa 55:1–5). All who hunger and thirst can look forward to that banquet that will celebrate the full union of Christ and his church.

Luke wrote his gospel and its sequel, the Acts of the Apostles, for an ever-expanding church. The community of disciples was extending "to the ends of the earth" (Acts 1:8), and Luke wrote to help the church transcend divisiveness and understand its universal character. Unlike our world of fast foods and instant meals, table fellowship in the world of Jesus expressed solidarity among people and created intimate relationships. The table of the Lord could tolerate no divisions between Jewish Christians and Gentile Christians, Palestinians and foreigners, wealthy and poor, slaves and free people, or women and men.

Immediately before his meal at the home of a leading Pharisee, Jesus proclaimed the universal nature of God's long-awaited banquet: "People will come from east and west, from north and south, and will eat in the kingdom of God" (13:29). During the meal, Jesus focused his teaching first on the attitudes and behaviors of the guests toward one another (verses 7-11) and then on those of the host (verses 12-14). The result is Jesus' declaration that those least expected to share in the kingdom's feast will in fact share in it, while in contrast, those most expected to be participants may very well be among those who will be excluded. The humility of seeking the last place assures the guests of experiencing a place of honor. Inviting the poor, the crippled, the lame, and the blind (verses 13, 21) aligns the meal with the mission and ministry of Jesus.

Jesus told the parable of the great dinner (verses 16-24) in response to a guest who exclaimed, "Blessed is anyone who will eat bread in the kingdom of God!" (verse 15). It is a parable about a meal told within the context of a meal. The Eucharist is a sacrament of God's kingdom, a manifestation in the present of what we all await. The church must be a sign of hope for all people, especially the sinner, the poor, and the outcast, and its Eucharist must be a visible expression and proclamation of that hope. Indeed, a Eucharist that reflects the divine generosity of Jesus reveals the kingdom of God in our midst.

Reflection and discussion

• What is the relationship between the future banquet of God's kingdom and the church's Eucharist?

• Why did Jesus do so much of his teaching around the dinner table?

• How does Jesus' teaching about the attitudes and behaviors of dinner hosts and guests challenge the way the church celebrates the Eucharist?

• What can I do about factions, exclusiveness, and lack of hospitality at the Sunday Eucharist of my church?

• Why must the church be a sign of hope for people? How can the Eucharist be a visible expression of that hope?

Prayer

Messiah and Lord, you prepare a feast and invite everyone from the least to the greatest, from the east to the west. Help me to respond to your generous invitation with complete acceptance. I trust in you to satisfy my hunger and thirst with your lavish grace.

I confer on you, just as my Father has conferred on me, a kingdom, so that you may eat and drink at my table in my kingdom. Luke 22:29–30

Feasting in the Kingdom of God

LUKE 22:14–30 *¹⁴When the hour came, he took his place at the table, and the apostles with him. ¹⁵He said to them, "I have eagerly desired to eat this Passover with you before I suffer; ¹⁶for I tell you, I will not eat it until it is fulfilled in the kingdom of God." ¹⁷Then he took a cup, and after giving thanks he said, "Take this and divide it among yourselves; ¹⁸for I tell you that from now on I will not drink of the fruit of the vine until the kingdom of God comes." ¹⁹Then he took a loaf of bread, and when he had given thanks, he broke it and gave it to them, saying, "This is my body, which is given for you. Do this in remembrance of me." ²⁰And he did the same with the cup after supper, saying, "This cup that is poured out for you is the new covenant in my blood.*

²¹But see, the one who betrays me is with me, and his hand is on the table. ²²For the Son of Man is going as it has been determined, but woe to that one by whom he is betrayed!" ²³Then they began to ask one another, which one of them it could be who would do this.

²⁴A dispute also arose among them as to which one of them was to be regarded as the greatest. ²⁵But he said to them, "The kings of the Gentiles lord it over them; and those in authority over them are called benefactors. ²⁶But not so with you; rather the greatest among you must become like the youngest, and the leader like one who serves. ²⁷For who is greater, the one who is at the table or the one

who serves? Is it not the one at the table? But I am among you as one who serves.
[28] *"You are those who have stood by me in my trials;* [29] *and I confer on you, just as my Father has conferred on me, a kingdom,* [30] *so that you may eat and drink at my table in my kingdom, and you will sit on thrones judging the twelve tribes of Israel."*

The Last Supper in Luke's gospel is the culmination of the series of meals that precedes it. What the passion and resurrection is to the ministry of Jesus, the Last Supper is to the previous meals with Jesus. All that Jesus has previously said and done is presented at the Last Supper in relationship to the dying and rising of Christ. As a result, Jesus gives his church a dramatically new kind of meal in which participants share in the great events of salvation. Luke demonstrates that the Last Supper is a Passover meal, and thus presents the Eucharist as a new Passover. The Jewish Passover was a sacred meal in which the Jewish people became part of the defining events of their history that made them a people. The Christian Passover is also a sacred meal in which followers of Jesus share in the passion and resurrection of Jesus. The ancient Passover of Israel freed God's people from bondage and passed that inheritance on to their children. The new Passover frees its participants from the slavery of sin and death, joining its participants to Christ and uniting them in the family of God, which includes its ancestors in Israel's history. Like the ancient Passover, it is a meal of remembrance and hope.

As the last meal of Jesus' historical life, the Last Supper is presented as Jesus' farewell discourse. Like all farewell speeches in the Bible, it is written to address future generations. Standing at the beginning of the passion account, Jesus' discourse interprets the saving events of his dying and rising, showing future Christians how to enter into this paschal mystery. He tells them, "Do this in remembrance of me" (verse 19), which means not only performing the eucharistic ritual and making present again the saving actions of Christ, but also making the same self-gift that Jesus made. The broken body "given for you" and the cup "poured out for you" (verses 19-20) is the body and blood of Christ, but in Eucharist it is also that of the church, uniting itself with the offering of Christ and giving itself as the sacrament of Christ's presence in the world.

The final discourse of Jesus shows how the Christian Eucharist not only brings the saving moments of the past into the present, but also how it anticipates the future. Jesus states that he will not eat the Passover again "until it is fulfilled in the kingdom of God" (verses 16, 18). Though Jesus was sharing the Last Supper of his historical life, he would again eat the supper and drink the cup with his apostles after the resurrection with the coming of the kingdom of God in the life of the church. In the Acts of the Apostles, Peter told the crowd that Jesus appeared to chosen witnesses "who ate and drank with him after he rose from the dead" (Acts 10:41). Fulfillment in the kingdom of God began with the apostolic church after the resurrection, and it looks forward to perfect completion in the last days. The church that celebrates the presence of the risen Christ in its Eucharist also prays "thy kingdom come" (11:2).

Luke placed the notice of Jesus' betrayal and the dispute among the apostles over who is the greatest after the meal (verses 21-27). As a chilling sequel to the Last Supper the words of Jesus speak to his church about how to live in the body of Christ, in the new covenant, in the kingdom of God. Just as betrayal and arrogant ambition occurred within the circle of the covenant meal, it will continue to occur within Christ's church. Jesus presents himself as the servant of the table and calls all who celebrate the Eucharist to do the same. Those who remain faithful to Jesus and celebrate the Lord's Supper in memory of him, will eat and drink at the table in Christ's kingdom (verse 30).

Reflection and discussion

• In what ways is the Last Supper a meal of both remembrance and hope?

• What are the different levels of meaning in the words of Jesus, "Do this in remembrance of me"?

• How will the Passover be "fulfilled in the kingdom of God" (verse 16)?

• How does Jesus challenge his future church in his final discourse (verses 21-27)? What does it mean to faithfully celebrate the Eucharist today?

Prayer

Lord Jesus, you have invited us to experience the saving mysteries of your death and resurrection for all times by celebrating the Eucharist. As I take your body and blood, renew your covenant within me so that I may unite my life in union with yours and give my life for others.

When he was at the table with them, he took bread, blessed and broke it, and gave it to them. Then their eyes were opened, and they recognized him; and he vanished from their sight. Luke 24:30–31

The Breaking of the Bread at Emmaus

LUKE 24:13–35 *¹³Now on that same day two of them were going to a village called Emmaus, about seven miles from Jerusalem, ¹⁴and talking with each other about all these things that had happened. ¹⁵While they were talking and discussing, Jesus himself came near and went with them, ¹⁶but their eyes were kept from recognizing him. ¹⁷And he said to them, "What are you discussing with each other while you walk along?" They stood still, looking sad. ¹⁸Then one of them, whose name was Cleopas, answered him, "Are you the only stranger in Jerusalem who does not know the things that have taken place there in these days?" ¹⁹He asked them, "What things?" They replied, "The things about Jesus of Nazareth, who was a prophet mighty in deed and word before God and all the people, ²⁰and how our chief priests and leaders handed him over to be condemned to death and crucified him. ²¹But we had hoped that he was the one to redeem Israel. Yes, and besides all this, it is now the third day since these things took place. ²²Moreover, some women of our group astounded us. They were at the tomb early this morning, ²³and when they did not find his body there, they came back and told us that they had indeed seen a vision of angels who said that he was alive. ²⁴Some of those who were with us went to the tomb and found it just as the women had said; but they did not see him." ²⁵Then he said to them, "Oh, how foolish you are,* *and how slow of heart to believe all that the prophets have declared! ²⁶ Was it not necessary that the Messiah should suffer these things and then enter into his glory?" ²⁷ Then beginning with Moses and all the prophets, he interpreted to them the things about himself in all the scriptures.*

²⁸ As they came near the village to which they were going, he walked ahead as if he were going on. ²⁹ But they urged him strongly, saying, "Stay with us, because it is almost evening and the day is now nearly over." So he went in to stay with them. ³⁰ When he was at the table with them, he took bread, blessed and broke it, and gave it to them. ³¹ Then their eyes were opened, and they recognized him; and he vanished from their sight. ³² They said to each other, "Were not our hearts burning within us while he was talking to us on the road, while he was opening the scriptures to us?" ³³ That same hour they got up and returned to Jerusalem; and they found the eleven and their companions gathered together. ³⁴ They were saying, "The Lord has risen indeed, and he has appeared to Simon!" ³⁵ Then they told what had happened on the road, and how he had been made known to them in the breaking of the bread.

The companions who met Jesus along the road to Emmaus were two of the chosen witnesses "who ate and drank with him after he rose from the dead" (Acts 10:41). The table fellowship that the disciples had experienced with Jesus before his death and resurrection continued afterward, but in a new way. The Emmaus account describes, in narrative form, the way the early Christians learned to experience the Risen Lord in their eucharistic assemblies.

When the day of resurrection was nearly over, the two disciples convinced Jesus to stay with them (verse 29). Reclining at table at the time of the evening meal, the guest became the host. When Jesus "took bread, blessed and broke it, and gave it" to his disciples, they recognized him (verses 30-31). His gestures look back to the action of the Last Supper and ahead to the "breaking of the bread" in the early church of the Acts of the Apostles.

As the narrative reaches its climax and Jesus then vanishes from their sight, the disciples realize that it was Christ's risen presence they were experiencing all along. They remembered that their hearts were burning with anticipation and love as Jesus interpreted the Scriptures for them (verse 32). Before they could recognize Jesus in the breaking of the bread, they had to first understand from the Scriptures how it was "necessary that the Messiah should suffer these things and then enter into his glory" (verse 26). The passion was Jesus' way into a new and glorified life, which did not remove him from them but allowed him to remain with them in a new, sacramental way.

The Emmaus account was written with the worship of the early church in mind. The disciples and Luke's readers now realize how the risen Lord will be present to his church. The account demonstrates the dynamic relationship between word and sacrament, and it reflects the twofold structure of the Christian assembly: the liturgy of the word and the liturgy of the Eucharist. Both the interpretation of the Scriptures and the breaking of the bread are actions of the risen Christ in which his presence is made real for the church.

But it is not only the liturgical action that suggests eucharistic worship; Eucharist is also experienced in the movement from table to witnessing to others. "That same hour" the disciples returned to Jerusalem to communicate their experience of how they came to know the risen Christ (verses 33-35). The narrative began with the disciples walking slowly and hopelessly from Jerusalem to Emmaus; it ends with their movement hurriedly and expectantly from Emmaus to Jerusalem. Once they had experienced Jesus alive, they could not keep the news to themselves. They joined their witness to that of Simon Peter and the believers in Jerusalem, communicating their experiences and becoming a worshiping and witnessing community of disciples. Likewise, those who participate in the church's Eucharist are sent forth to be evangelizers—to spread the gospel and imbue society with Christian values.

Reflection and discussion

• What indicates that Luke wrote this account in the context of Christian worship? What does the narrative instruct the church about its celebration of Eucharist?

• Why does the liturgy of the word always come before the church's eucharistic prayer at the altar? In what way does coming to understand the Scriptures help me to understand the presence of Christ in Eucharist?

• What is necessary on my part in order to recognize the presence of the Risen Lord in Eucharist?

• What is the relationship between Eucharist and evangelization? Why must a worshiping community become a witnessing community?

Prayer

Glorified Christ, open the Scriptures to me, so that you may also open my eyes, mind, and heart to you. Walk with me along the road of life and teach me to recognize your risen and living presence in the celebration of Eucharist.

On the first day of the week, when we met to break bread,
Paul was holding a discussion with them; since he intended to leave the
next day, he continued speaking until midnight. Acts 20:7

A Growing Church Devoted to Breaking the Bread

ACTS 2:42–47 *⁴²They devoted themselves to the apostles' teaching and fellowship, to the breaking of bread and the prayers. ⁴³Awe came upon everyone, because many wonders and signs were being done by the apostles. ⁴⁴All who believed were together and had all things in common; ⁴⁵they would sell their possessions and goods and distribute the proceeds to all, as any had need. ⁴⁶Day by day, as they spent much time together in the temple, they broke bread at home and ate their food with glad and generous hearts, ⁴⁷praising God and having the goodwill of all the people. And day by day the Lord added to their number those who were being saved.*

ACTS 20:7–12 *⁷On the first day of the week, when we met to break bread, Paul was holding a discussion with them; since he intended to leave the next day, he continued speaking until midnight. ⁸There were many lamps in the room upstairs where we were meeting. ⁹A young man named Eutychus, who was sitting in the window, began to sink off into a deep sleep while Paul talked still longer. Overcome by sleep, he fell to the ground three floors below and was picked* *up dead. [10]But Paul went down, and bending over him took him in his arms, and said, "Do not be alarmed, for his life is in him." [11]Then Paul went upstairs, and after he had broken bread and eaten, he continued to converse with them until dawn; then he left. [12]Meanwhile they had taken the boy away alive and were not a little comforted.*

Because the Acts of the Apostles is a sequel to Luke's gospel, we see the strong relationship between the development of the Eucharist in the apostolic church and its origin in the ministry of Jesus. "The breaking of the bread," as the Eucharist is called in Luke's writings, is closely connected to the many meals that Jesus ate with his disciples, especially their culmination in the Last Supper and the Supper at Emmaus. The apostles remembered and obeyed Jesus' instructions at the Last Supper, "Do this in remembrance of me." At Emmaus, the disciples reported that Jesus "had been made known to them in the breaking of the bread" (Luke 24:35) on the day of resurrection, "the first day of the week" (Luke 24:1, 13). After Pentecost the church continued to celebrate the breaking of the bread and continued to experience the presence of the risen Lord in that weekly event. From the beginning, the Eucharist bound the disciples together in a new community of faith.

In a summary passage in Acts, Luke presents four key elements of the church's life in its infancy: "the apostles' teaching and fellowship, the breaking of bread and the prayers" (2:42). Because the disciples "devoted themselves" to these four distinguishing marks, the church continued to grow and its members experienced salvation (2:47). Devotion to "the apostles' teaching" meant faithfully listening to the teachings of Jesus handed on by the apostles to their community. It also meant handing on the word to others, teaching as the apostles taught, and devoting themselves to the ministry of the word. The "fellowship" or "communion" suggests the bond of responsibility the believers experienced for one another through their union together in Christ.

The fellowship in Christ found its highest expression when the community gathered for "the breaking of the bread." There the teachings of the apostles were savored and reflected upon in the context of the communal life. The church's breaking of the bread is not just any bread; it is "the bread." It is "the bread" prefigured when Jesus broke the bread and gave it to his apostles to feed the hungry crowd of thousands. With the twelve baskets of bread left over, the twelve apostles continued to break the bread to feed thousands more with the bread of God's kingdom. It is "the bread" that Jesus broke at the Last Supper saying, "This is my body which is given for you." It is "the bread" Jesus broke with the disciples at Emmaus, which opened their eyes and enabled them to recognize their Risen Lord.

"The prayers" refer to the church's practice of saying prayers at set times during the day. This began as the disciples continued their Jewish practice of participating in public prayer at the temple at set hours (Acts 3:1). We learn from the Old Testament that a devout Jew prayed three times a day—at evening, morning, and noon—facing Jerusalem (Psalm 55:17; Daniel 6:10). The daily prayer of the church soon consisted of the psalms and a thrice-daily praying of the Our Father. The prayers of the church flowed from their "fellowship" and led up to their weekly Eucharist on the Lord's day.

While the Eucharist was at the heart of the church's life, the account of Paul's departure from the church in Troas is the only narrative of an actual eucharistic assembly in the New Testament (20:7–12). The account takes place "on the first day of the week," when the community "met to break bread." In Acts, the first day of the week was the day when Christians proclaimed the resurrection of Jesus and celebrated his eucharistic presence with them. Because Sunday was a working day in the Jewish and Roman world, the church met in the evening for their weekly Eucharist. It seems that the early Christians also "broke bread" daily in smaller groups in their homes (2:46), but it was on the Lord's day that the whole church assembled for their Eucharist. The first day of the week expressed the experience of Christ's resurrection as the first day of the new creation. The Christians knew they participated in God's new creation through the breaking of the bread of God's kingdom.

The account is included in Acts because of Paul's departure from the community and the marvelous healing of Eutychus. The young man's unfortunate fall from the third floor was the result of the late hour and the many oil lamps that depleted the oxygen from the room in which the church was meeting (20:8–9). Having heard the word and participated in the Eucharist, the community was able to take the young man away alive (20:11–12). There was no reason to grieve. Participating in the new creation, they were all comforted beyond measure.

Reflection and discussion

• In what ways do I participate in the four key elements of the church's life today?

• What is the significance of the fact that the church celebrates its primary Eucharist on the first day of the week?

• What have I learned about the origins and development of the Eucharist from the writings of Luke?

Prayer

Risen and Glorified Lord, you are the Living One, found among the living. You invite me to participate in the new creation through my sharing your Eucharist. Fill me with your Holy Spirit of Pentecost so that I may be devoted to the teachings, prayers, communion, and Eucharist of your church.

SUGGESTIONS FOR FACILITATORS, GROUP SESSION 5

1. Welcome group members and ask if anyone has any questions, announcements, or requests.

2. You may want to pray this prayer as a group:

Savior and Lord, through the inspired writings of Matthew and Luke, you teach us about your kingdom and the riches you want us to share. In Eucharist you offer us forgiveness, nourishment, healing, and hope. You share your very life with us and help us anticipate the banquet of life that lasts forever. Through the teachings, prayers, fellowship, and Eucharist of your church, you motive us and empower us to be your witnesses in the world. Keep us faithful to your word and dedicated to your sacraments.

3. Ask one or more of the following questions:
   - What insight from the gospels most inspired you from this week's study?
   - What new understanding of the Eucharist stands out for you this week?

4. Discuss lessons 19 through 24. Choose one or more of the questions for reflection and discussion from each lesson to talk over as a group.

5. Ask the group members to name one thing they have most appreciated about the way the group has worked during this Bible study. Ask group members to discuss any changes they might suggest in the way the group functions in future studies.

6. Invite group members to complete lessons 25 through 30 on their own during the six days before the next meeting. They should write out their own answers to the questions as preparation for next week's session.

7. Ask the group how this study is affecting the way they participate in the Sunday Eucharist.

8. Conclude by praying aloud together the prayer at the end of one of the lessons discussed. You may want to end the prayer by asking members to voice prayers of thanksgiving.

"Those who eat my flesh and drink my blood have eternal life,
and I will raise them up on the last day;
for my flesh is true food and my blood is true drink." John 6:54–55

The Bread of Life for the Life of the World

JOHN 6:41–59 *⁴¹Then the Jews began to complain about him because he said, "I am the bread that came down from heaven." ⁴²They were saying, "Is not this Jesus, the son of Joseph, whose father and mother we know? How can he now say, 'I have come down from heaven'?" ⁴³Jesus answered them, "Do not complain among yourselves. ⁴⁴No one can come to me unless drawn by the Father who sent me; and I will raise that person up on the last day. ⁴⁵It is written in the prophets, 'And they shall all be taught by God.' Everyone who has heard and learned from the Father comes to me. ⁴⁶Not that anyone has seen the Father except the one who is from God; he has seen the Father. ⁴⁷Very truly, I tell you, whoever believes has eternal life. ⁴⁸I am the bread of life. ⁴⁹Your ancestors ate the manna in the wilderness, and they died. ⁵⁰This is the bread that comes down from heaven, so that one may eat of it and not die. ⁵¹I am the living bread that came down from heaven. Whoever eats of this bread will live forever; and the bread that I will give for the life of the world is my flesh."*

⁵²The Jews then disputed among themselves, saying, "How can this man give us his flesh to eat?" ⁵³So Jesus said to them, "Very truly, I tell you, unless you eat the flesh of the Son of Man and drink his blood, you have no life in you. ⁵⁴Those who eat my flesh and drink my blood have eternal life, and I will raise them up on the last day; [55] *for my flesh is true food and my blood is true drink.* [56] *Those who eat my flesh and drink my blood abide in me, and I in them.* [57] *Just as the living Father sent me, and I live because of the Father, so whoever eats me will live because of me.* [58] *This is the bread that came down from heaven, not like that which your ancestors ate, and they died. But the one who eats this bread will live forever."* [59] *He said these things while he was teaching in the synagogue at Capernaum.*

T he entire gospel of John demonstrates how the eternal, life-giving Word of God "became flesh and lived among us" in the person of Jesus (1:14). The Eucharist in John is the sacramental presence of this Word become flesh. The eternal Word not only dwells with us but gives himself as our life-giving food: "The bread that I will give for the life of the world is my flesh" (verse 51). In the other gospels and in Paul's writings the Eucharist is primarily related to Christ's death and resurrection; in John's gospel, the Eucharist is primarily related to the Incarnation, the Word of God made flesh. Through the Eucharist, believers are invited to become one with Christ, as he and the Father are one, and through that intimate unity, to experience eternal life (verse 57).

Rather than connecting the Eucharist to the Last Supper as the final mandate of Jesus, John's gospel places references to it throughout Jesus' life. In this way he shows that the Eucharist flows from everything Jesus said and did as the Word made flesh. The most important eucharistic passages of the gospel are found in the sixth chapter, in which Jesus satisfies the hungry crowd with the loaves of bread and then proclaims himself as "the bread of life" that truly nourishes and satisfies humanity's deepest hungers.

Jesus' discourse on the bread of life can be divided into two interrelated parts. The first is about the bread that Jesus is, the true bread from heaven (verses 25-50). The second concerns the bread Jesus gives, his flesh for the life of the world (verses 51-58). The first part is about the bread the Father gave, Jesus' very person coming down from heaven to give life to the world. The second concerns the bread Jesus himself gave, his eucharistic flesh that gives everlasting life to those who receive it. The gift cannot be separated from the giver; Jesus, the Word made flesh, gives his flesh as Eucharist.

The words of Jesus are deeply rooted in the Scriptures of Israel. He contrasts the bread their ancestors ate, the bread Moses provided in the wilderness, with the bread from heaven that Jesus provides, "the living bread that came down from heaven" (verses 49-51). Jesus also contrasts the Old Testament banquet, in which Wisdom offers the invitation to "eat of my bread and drink of the wine" (Prov 9:5), with the banquet of his own flesh and blood (verses 54-56). When people taste of Wisdom, they hunger and thirst for more (Sir 24:21), but Jesus, the Wisdom of God incarnate, offers a food that satisfies humanity's hunger and thirst completely.

Sharing in the Eucharist, like sharing in the mystery of Christ's death and resurrection, is at the heart of Christian life. Partaking of Christ's eucharistic presence is the means to participate in the life God offers us: "Those who eat my flesh and drink my blood have eternal life" (verse 54). The Eucharist is an intimate sharing in the real presence of Christ in a way that is truly human and truly divine: "For my flesh is true food and my blood true drink" (verse 55). The Word of God made flesh has become Eucharist. The Eucharist is the sacramental climax of the mission of the Word of God to the world.

Reflection and discussion

• In what way is John's eucharistic theology focused on the Incarnation, the Word made flesh?

• In what ways does this eucharistic discourse focus on the real presence of Christ in the church's Eucharist?

• How does "I am the bread of life" indicate that Jesus is both the giver and the gift? What is the gift that Jesus gives?

• Which verse most convinces me that Jesus is really present in his gift of the Eucharist?

• How can partaking in the Eucharist lead me to a deeper, more intimate relationship with Jesus Christ?

Prayer

Lord Jesus, in the sacrament of the Eucharist you give your body as my food and your blood as my drink. Deepen my awareness of your living presence as I share in the Eucharist, and help me to use every opportunity to draw closer to you.

Jesus asked the twelve, "Do you also wish to go away?"
Simon Peter answered him, "Lord, to whom can we go?
You have the words of eternal life." John 6:67–68

Accepting the Words of Eternal Life

JOHN 6:60–71 *60When many of his disciples heard it, they said, "This teaching is difficult; who can accept it?" 61But Jesus, being aware that his disciples were complaining about it, said to them, "Does this offend you? 62Then what if you were to see the Son of Man ascending to where he was before? 63It is the spirit that gives life; the flesh is useless. The words that I have spoken to you are spirit and life. 64But among you there are some who do not believe." For Jesus knew from the first who were the ones that did not believe, and who was the one that would betray him. 65And he said, "For this reason I have told you that no one can come to me unless it is granted by the Father."*

66Because of this many of his disciples turned back and no longer went about with him. 67So Jesus asked the twelve, "Do you also wish to go away?" 68Simon Peter answered him, "Lord, to whom can we go? You have the words of eternal life. 69We have come to believe and know that you are the Holy One of God." 70Jesus answered them, "Did I not choose you, the twelve? Yet one of you is a devil." 71He was speaking of Judas son of Simon Iscariot, for he, though one of the twelve, was going to betray him.

After Jesus fed the hungry crowds, the people proclaimed him as "the prophet who is to come" and they were ready to carry him away and "make him king" (6:14–15). Yet, as Jesus offered his discourse on the bread of life, the crowd moved from acclamation to confusion to hostility (verses 41, 52). Accepting Jesus as coming from heaven to offer himself as the world's nourishment and source of eternal life demanded a leap of faith that most in the crowd chose not to make. The tension that formed between Jesus and the crowd introduced the hostility that led to his crucifixion (7:1).

As the crowd dispersed, Jesus is left with his disciples. They complain, "This teaching is difficult," and they wonder how anyone could accept it (verse 60). At this point, the teachings of Jesus had become so crucial that they demanded a personal decision. Some of his disciples did not believe (verse 64); they left him and returned to their former way of life (verse 66). But when Jesus turned to the twelve and asked, "Do you also wish to go away?" (verse 67), Simon Peter expressed words of faith in Jesus. Because they had come to trust that Jesus is "the Holy One of God," they were able to accept his eucharistic message as "the words of eternal life" (verses 68-69).

At the time John's gospel was written, there were some groups denying the physical humanity of Christ. In reaction to them, John's community emphasized the fact that Jesus lived a truly human life and that in him God's Word had become flesh. This emphasis on the Incarnation carried over to John's emphasis on the real presence of Christ in the Eucharist. It is as the Word made flesh that Jesus died, rose, is glorified, and is now present to us in sacrament. Physically eating and drinking the sacramental flesh and blood of Christ in Eucharist joins the believer to him in the most intimate way.

Though John's gospel explained the amazing sacramental synthesis of Word and flesh, it was not easy to maintain spirit and flesh in delicate balance. Jesus did indeed give his flesh for the life of the world, and consuming his flesh brings us eternal life. But to understand and accept that teaching, human flesh is of no benefit (verse 63). Since the words of Jesus are "spirit and life," the disciples needed the Spirit who gives life to receive those words. The human response is fragile. While the faith of Simon Peter is admirable, the challenge comes as faith is tested. The question of Jesus as he watched many of his followers turn away is addressed to us in every age, "Do you also wish to go away?"

Reflection and discussion

• Why is the teaching of Jesus in John 6 so difficult to accept (verse 60)?

• What does Jesus ask of me as I eat his body and drink his blood?

• When have I been most aware of Jesus' presence in the Eucharist and felt in deepest personal contact with him?

Prayer

Lord of Life, I have come to believe that you are the Holy One of God and that you have the words of eternal life. Thank you for inviting me to share deeply in your life by eating your flesh as true food and drinking your blood as true drink.

If I, your Lord and Teacher, have washed your feet, you also ought to wash one another's feet. For I have set you an example, that you also should do as I have done to you. John 13:14–15

Imitating the Love of Jesus

JOHN 13:1–30 ¹*Now before the festival of the Passover, Jesus knew that his hour had come to depart from this world and go to the Father. Having loved his own who were in the world, he loved them to the end. ²The devil had already put it into the heart of Judas son of Simon Iscariot to betray him. And during supper ³Jesus, knowing that the Father had given all things into his hands, and that he had come from God and was going to God, ⁴got up from the table, took off his outer robe, and tied a towel around himself. ⁵Then he poured water into a basin and began to wash the disciples' feet and to wipe them with the towel that was tied around him. ⁶He came to Simon Peter, who said to him, "Lord, are you going to wash my feet?" ⁷Jesus answered, "You do not know now what I am doing, but later you will understand." ⁸Peter said to him, "You will never wash my feet." Jesus answered, "Unless I wash you, you have no share with me." ⁹Simon Peter said to him, "Lord, not my feet only but also my hands and my head!" ¹⁰Jesus said to him, "One who has bathed does not need to wash, except for the feet, but is entirely clean. And you are clean, though not all of you." ¹¹For he knew who was to betray him; for this reason he said, "Not all of you are clean."*

¹²After he had washed their feet, had put on his robe, and had returned to the table, he said to them, "Do you know what I have done to you? ¹³You call me Teacher and Lord—and you are right, for that is what I am. ¹⁴So if I, your Lord and Teacher, have washed your feet, you also ought to wash one another's feet.

¹⁵*For I have set you an example, that you also should do as I have done to you.* ¹⁶*Very truly, I tell you, servants are not greater than their master, nor are messengers greater than the one who sent them.* ¹⁷*If you know these things, you are blessed if you do them.* ¹⁸*I am not speaking of all of you; I know whom I have chosen. But it is to fulfill the scripture, 'The one who ate my bread has lifted his heel against me.'* ¹⁹*I tell you this now, before it occurs, so that when it does occur, you may believe that I am he.* ²⁰*Very truly, I tell you, whoever receives one whom I send receives me; and whoever receives me receives him who sent me."*

²¹*After saying this Jesus was troubled in spirit, and declared, "Very truly, I tell you, one of you will betray me."* ²²*The disciples looked at one another, uncertain of whom he was speaking.* ²³*One of his disciples—the one whom Jesus loved— was reclining next to him;* ²⁴*Simon Peter therefore motioned to him to ask Jesus of whom he was speaking.* ²⁵*So while reclining next to Jesus, he asked him, "Lord, who is it?"* ²⁶*Jesus answered, "It is the one to whom I give this piece of bread when I have dipped it in the dish." So when he had dipped the piece of bread, he gave it to Judas son of Simon Iscariot.* ²⁷*After he received the piece of bread, Satan entered into him. Jesus said to him, "Do quickly what you are going to do."* ²⁸*Now no one at the table knew why he said this to him.* ²⁹*Some thought that, because Judas had the common purse, Jesus was telling him, "Buy what we need for the festival"; or, that he should give something to the poor.* ³⁰*So, after receiving the piece of bread, he immediately went out. And it was night.*

The washing of the disciples' feet is narrated in John's gospel during the Last Supper. It takes places as the transition between the seven signs given by Jesus and his departure to the Father through his passion, death, and resurrection. The symbolic action of washing the feet of his disciples summarizes the meaning of Jesus' entire life and death as an act of love: "Having loved his own who were in the world, he loved them to the end" (verse 1). "To the end" means both to the end of his life on earth, and loving them completely.

In place of the institution of the Eucharist, recounted during the Last Supper in the other gospels, John's gospel recounts Jesus washing the feet of his disciples. Both actions express the self-giving of Jesus and his love "to the end." John did not include the words of institution over the bread and wine in his gospel because these words had already been integrated into the weekly Eucharist of his community. Instead John decided to express the meaning of Eucharist, namely through the bread of life discourse of chapter six and the washing of the feet and the discourse that follows of John's Last Supper account. Since the gospel was written for the believing community and read during their weekly Eucharist, the worshipping assembly would listen to the gospel in the liturgy of the Word and then listen to the words of Jesus over the bread and wine in the liturgy of the Eucharist. In this way, the liturgical assembly would gain a richer understanding of Eucharist at the table of both word and sacrament.

Jesus' washing of the feet was not the same as giving his body and blood, but it brought out an important dimension of its meaning. Jesus totally gave himself in service to others, in sacrificial love "to the end," and he asked his disciples to do the same. His eucharistic words in the other gospels, "Do this in memory of me," culminate in the Eucharist, but extend to his whole life so that we may imitate the entire example he set for us. In John's gospel, Jesus asks us to model our lives on the pattern of his life: "For I have set you an example, that you also should do as I have done to you" (verse 15). We are to love "to the end"—to the end of our lives and as completely as we can love.

The eucharistic assembly would have listened to the proclamation of this dramatic gesture of Jesus and understood it as a symbolic expression of the Word made flesh, the humiliation of the divine Word that took place in the Incarnation. Jesus taking off his outer garments reminded the assembly of the moment his garments would be forcibly taken from him (19:23–24), and he would be left to die hanging from the cross. The close bond between Eucharist and humble service challenges every eucharistic assembly to ponder the action of Jesus, who gave his flesh for the life of the world, and to ask ourselves whether we are truly following the "example" Jesus left us.

Reflection and discussion

• What is the connection between footwashing and the Holy Thursday? Why is footwashing retained in the Holy Week liturgy?

• What dimension of the meaning of Eucharist is brought out through the washing of disciples' feet?

• In what way does the celebration of Eucharist challenge the Christian assembly to respond to the genuine needs of those around them.

• In what way am I called to imitate the loving service of Jesus "to the end"?

Prayer

Suffering Servant, you loved your disciples to the end. Help me to love as you loved, to serve as you served, and to give myself as you gave yourself completely. As I share your body and blood, help me to respond to the physical and spiritual hungers and thirsts of your people.

I am the vine, you are the branches. Those who abide in me and I in them bear much fruit, because apart from me you can do nothing. John 15:5

Remaining United with the True Vine

JOHN 15:1–17 *¹"I am the true vine, and my Father is the vinegrower. ²He removes every branch in me that bears no fruit. Every branch that bears fruit he prunes to make it bear more fruit. ³You have already been cleansed by the word that I have spoken to you. ⁴Abide in me as I abide in you. Just as the branch cannot bear fruit by itself unless it abides in the vine, neither can you unless you abide in me. ⁵I am the vine, you are the branches. Those who abide in me and I in them bear much fruit, because apart from me you can do nothing. ⁶Whoever does not abide in me is thrown away like a branch and withers; such branches are gathered, thrown into the fire, and burned. ⁷If you abide in me, and my words abide in you, ask for whatever you wish, and it will be done for you. ⁸My Father is glorified by this, that you bear much fruit and become my disciples.*

⁹As the Father has loved me, so I have loved you; abide in my love. ¹⁰If you keep my commandments, you will abide in my love, just as I have kept my Father's commandments and abide in his love. ¹¹I have said these things to you so that my joy may be in you, and that your joy may be complete.

¹²"This is my commandment, that you love one another as I have loved you. ¹³No one has greater love than this, to lay down one's life for one's friends. ¹⁴You are my friends if you do what I command you. ¹⁵I do not call you servants any longer, because the servant does not know what the master is doing; but I have called you friends, because I have made known to you everything that I have heard from my Father. ¹⁶You did not choose me but I chose you. And I appointed you to go and bear fruit, fruit that will last, so that the Father will give you whatever you ask him in my name. ¹⁷I am giving you these commands so that you may love one another.

Since Jesus' discourse on the vine and the branches is given at the Last Supper, it may be seen as the cup parallel to the bread of life discourse of John 6. Jesus' statement, "I am the true vine" (verse 1), parallels his declaration in the previous discourse, "I am the bread of life." Together they are used by John to develop the eucharistic teaching of his gospel. Wine is the "fruit of the vine" according to the Jewish prayer used to bless the wine at festival meals like the Last Supper. Like the image of the loaves, the vine became a eucharistic symbol in the writings and art of the early church.

When Jesus says he is the true vine, he is referring back to an Old Testament image of a vine God has planted (Ps 80:8; Jer 2:21; Isa 5:1–7). The vine in these passages is Israel, so when Jesus applies the vine image to himself and his followers, he is saying that all those who belong to him are the new people of God. The image emphasizes that Jesus is the source of life, as in his discourse on the bread of life, and that everyone who remains united with him shares in his life. Notice that Jesus is not the trunk of the vine, but the vine as a whole. His disciples are the branches that make up the vine. They receive life from him not by being merely connected to him; they share in his life by becoming part of him. Jesus not only gives life to his followers; he lives his life in them, so that they are fully united with him and live in him. We experience this intimate unity with Jesus through sharing his life in Eucharist. When we are so united with Christ, we actually live with his life and love with his love.

The source of this life and love is the Father, the vine-grower. As a wise vine-grower he knows that a vine requires careful pruning to be fruitful. Vines allowed to grow without pruning will produce smaller and smaller grapes as the vines gradually return to their wild state. The pruning represents the trials and suffering in the lives of those who unite their lives with the loving and total sacrifice of Jesus. The image is similar to "drinking the cup" in Mark's gospel. The greatest love is "to lay down one's life for one's friends" (verse 13), the self-giving love demonstrated by Jesus at the Last Supper and on the cross. Being united with Jesus through the Eucharist means offering our lives in union with his and bearing the fruit of loving service.

Reflection and discussion

• In what way does the image of the vine express the unity I experience with Christ in the Eucharist? How does it express the unity I experience with others in Eucharist?

• What is the greatest form of love (verse 13)? How does receiving the Eucharist help me to offer self-giving love to others?

• What fruit am I producing because my life is intimately united with Jesus?

Prayer

Fruitful Vine, keep me connected to you so that I may bear the fruit of loving service for your people. Thank you for the great love you showed in laying down your life in sacrifice, and help me unite my sufferings with your sacrifice on the altar.

Now it was the day of Preparation for the Passover; and it was about noon.

John 19:14

The Lamb of God, Our Passover Sacrifice

JOHN 19:13–37 *¹³When Pilate heard these words, he brought Jesus outside and sat on the judge's bench at a place called The Stone Pavement, or in Hebrew Gabbatha. ¹⁴Now it was the day of Preparation for the Passover; and it was about noon. He said to the Jews, "Here is your King!" ¹⁵They cried out, "Away with him! Away with him! Crucify him!" Pilate asked them, "Shall I crucify your King?" The chief priests answered, "We have no king but the emperor." ¹⁶Then he handed him over to them to be crucified.*

So they took Jesus; ¹⁷and carrying the cross by himself, he went out to what is called The Place of the Skull, which in Hebrew is called Golgotha. ¹⁸There they crucified him, and with him two others, one on either side, with Jesus between them.

¹⁹Pilate also had an inscription written and put on the cross. It read, "Jesus of Nazareth, the King of the Jews." ²⁰Many of the Jews read this inscription, because the place where Jesus was crucified was near the city; and it was written in Hebrew, in Latin, and in Greek. ²¹Then the chief priests of the Jews said to Pilate, "Do not write, 'The King of the Jews,' but, 'This man said, I am King of the Jews.'" ²²Pilate answered, "What I have written I have written." ²³When the soldiers had crucified Jesus, they took his clothes and divided them into four parts, one for each soldier. They also took his tunic; now the tunic was seamless, woven in one piece from the top. ²⁴*So they said to one another, "Let us not tear it, but cast lots for it to see who will get it." This was to fulfill what the scripture says, "They divided my clothes among themselves, and for my clothing they cast lots."* ²⁵*And that is what the soldiers did.*

Meanwhile, standing near the cross of Jesus were his mother, and his mother's sister, Mary the wife of Clopas, and Mary Magdalene. ²⁶*When Jesus saw his mother and the disciple whom he loved standing beside her, he said to his mother, "Woman, here is your son."* ²⁷*Then he said to the disciple, "Here is your mother." And from that hour the disciple took her into his own home.*

²⁸*After this, when Jesus knew that all was now finished, he said (in order to fulfill the scripture), "I am thirsty."* ²⁹*A jar full of sour wine was standing there. So they put a sponge full of the wine on a branch of hyssop and held it to his mouth.* ³⁰*When Jesus had received the wine, he said, "It is finished." Then he bowed his head and gave up his spirit.*

³¹*Since it was the day of Preparation, the Jews did not want the bodies left on the cross during the sabbath, especially because that sabbath was a day of great solemnity. So they asked Pilate to have the legs of the crucified men broken and the bodies removed.* ³²*Then the soldiers came and broke the legs of the first and of the other who had been crucified with him.* ³³*But when they came to Jesus and saw that he was already dead, they did not break his legs.* ³⁴*Instead, one of the soldiers pierced his side with a spear, and at once blood and water came out.* ³⁵*(He who saw this has testified so that you also may believe. His testimony is true, and he knows that he tells the truth.)* ³⁶*These things occurred so that the scripture might be fulfilled, "None of his bones shall be broken."* ³⁷*And again another passage of scripture says, "They will look on the one whom they have pierced."*

Though John's gospel does not explicitly include the institution of the Eucharist, he weaves eucharistic symbols of the Passover throughout his account. The Passover is the context of Jesus' bread of life discourse (6:4), the Last Supper and foot washing (13:1), and the sacrifice of Jesus on the cross (19:14). In all of these, John wants to emphasize that Jesus fulfilled the Passover sacrifice and meal in his own saving acts.

John's gospel has prepared the reader for this Passover imagery by announcing that Jesus is "the Lamb of God who takes away the sin of the world" (1:29). As Jesus is being handed over to death by Pilate, the gospel proclaimed that it was the day of Preparation for the Passover at about noon (verse 14)—the very hour when the sacrifice of the Passover lambs began in Jerusalem. The true Lamb of God will be sacrificed at the very moment the Passover lambs are sacrificed in the temple.

John also finds other ways to weave symbols of the Passover into this account. Immediately before his death on the cross, a sponge full of wine is lifted to Jesus on a stalk of hyssop (verse 29), the same plant the Israelites once used to place the blood of the Passover lamb on the doorframes of their homes. The sponge of wine is a brutal response to the earlier question of Jesus, "Am I not to drink of the cup that the Father has given me?" (18:11). After drinking the wine, Jesus said, "It is finished" (verse 30), "passing over" through his death and triumphantly concluding the saving task that had been given to him. After the death of Jesus, John also makes special note of the fact that his legs were not broken (verses 31-33), as was often done to hasten the death of a crucified victim. Since Exodus had commanded that the lamb's bones must not be broken (Exod 12:46), this detail is yet another sign that Jesus is the true Passover sacrifice, the Lamb of God. Through all of these connections to Passover, John ties together the Eucharist and the death of Jesus. His death on the cross is the Passover of our liberation. We unite ourselves to his saving death when we eat and drink the eucharistic sacrifice.

The final image offered to us immediately after the death of Jesus on the cross is the flow of blood and water from his pierced side (verse 34). Not only does the writer include this as a historical detail, but he testifies to its truth so that we may believe (verse 35). The early church saw the blood and water as symbols of Eucharist and baptism, the sacramental life of the church flowing from its Savior's side. The passage quoted from Zechariah about the side of the Messiah being pierced (verse 37; Zech 12:10) leads into a promise of a fountain bursting forth for the cleansing of sin (Zech 13:1). When we share in the sacramental life of Christ's church and receive the Eucharist, we drink from a fountain of life that springs forth from the side of our crucified Lord.

Reflection and discussion

• In what ways does John's gospel declare that Jesus is the true Passover Lamb?

• In what way does John's gospel indicate that celebrating the Eucharist is a participation in the liberating new Passover?

• Why is the blood and water flowing from the pierced side of Christ a hopeful symbol for me?

Prayer

Lamb of God, who takes away the sins of the world, have mercy on me. Your sacrificial death on the cross is the source of life for your church. As I feed on your Eucharist, help me to live confidently and victoriously in you.

"Worthy is the Lamb that was slaughtered to receive power and wealth and wisdom and might and honor and glory and blessing!" Rev 5:12

All Creation Worships the Lamb

REVELATION 5:6–14 *⁶Then I saw between the throne and the four living creatures and among the elders a Lamb standing as if it had been slaughtered, having seven horns and seven eyes, which are the seven spirits of God sent out into all the earth. ⁷He went and took the scroll from the right hand of the one who was seated on the throne. ⁸When he had taken the scroll, the four living creatures and the twenty-four elders fell before the Lamb, each holding a harp and golden bowls full of incense, which are the prayers of the saints. ⁹They sing a new song:*

"You are worthy to take the scroll
and to open its seals,
for you were slaughtered and by your blood you ransomed for God
saints from every tribe and language and people and nation;
¹⁰you have made them to be a kingdom and priests serving our God,
and they will reign on earth."

¹¹Then I looked, and I heard the voice of many angels surrounding the throne and the living creatures and the elders; they numbered myriads of myriads and thousands of thousands, ¹²singing with full voice,

"Worthy is the Lamb that was slaughtered
to receive power and wealth and wisdom and might
and honor and glory and blessing!"

¹³ *Then I heard every creature in heaven and on earth and under the earth and in the sea, and all that is in them, singing,*

"To the one seated on the throne and to the Lamb
be blessing and honor and glory and might
forever and ever!"

¹⁴ *And the four living creatures said, "Amen!" And the elders fell down and worshiped.*

The book of Revelation takes us beyond our earthly experience to contemplate the eternal realities of heaven. John, the visionary of the book, is granted "on the Lord's day" a vision of divine realities that are normally beyond our sight (1:9–11). He sees a Lamb that has been slaughtered standing before the throne of God (verse 6). The Lamb is standing alive before God, but it is visibly evident that he has been put to death. The Lamb is the crucified and risen Christ, the Lamb of God, whom all the lambs of sacrifice in the Old Testament prefigured. He is upright because "standing" is the ancient Christian position of the resurrection and the posture of Israelite priests. But at the same time he is showing the Father his wounds, presenting the fact that he has died and given his life in exchange for the life of the world. Since seven represents divine completion, the Lamb's seven horns and seven eyes express his divine power and divine knowledge. The seven spirits of God reveal that God's Lamb possesses the Holy Spirit and sends that Spirit to all people.

What John sees is the timeless sacrifice of Jesus being offered eternally to the Father. It is the constant worship of God in the heavenly liturgy in which the angels and saints and all creation participate. The blood of the Lamb is the offering that surpasses all others, the one sacrifice that makes people of every language and nation "a kingdom and priests serving our God" (verse 9). In relationship to God, the Lamb is the perfect priest offering himself in sacrifice. In relationship to us, he is the atonement for our sins and the source of new and eternal life.

Whenever we celebrate the Eucharist on earth we become part of the eternal adoration John describes in this vision. We worship God together with people throughout the world, united with all the creatures of heaven enjoying the fullness of God's presence. What John was able to glimpse directly is still veiled from our eyes, though it is no less real for us. Every Eucharist, no matter how small or obscure, has a universal character. It unites earth and heaven, embracing all of creation. The Eucharist calls us to become promoters of solidarity and justice, so that through God's grace and our cooperation, our world might reflect the heavenly communion of all God's creatures. As people who share in the Eucharist we take on the task of building a world more in harmony with God's plan, so that God's will might be done on earth as it is in heaven.

Reflection and discussion

• What does John's vision teach me about my participation in the Eucharist?

• In what sense is the Eucharist never a totally local experience?

• What does the vision of Revelation challenge me to do in order to promote solidarity among the people of God's creation?

Prayer

Eternal Priest and perfect Sacrifice, you are worthy to receive blessing, honor, power, and glory forever. Thank you for allowing me to share in your timeless sacrifice to the Father through the gift of the Eucharist.

SUGGESTIONS FOR FACILITATORS, GROUP SESSION 6

1. Welcome group members and make any final announcements or requests.

2. You may want to pray this prayer as a group:

Crucified and Risen Lord, you are the Bread of Life, the True Vine, and the slain and glorified Lamb. You invite us to share in the fruits of your eternal sacrifice to the Father by participating in your gift of Eucharist. You promise that we who eat your body and drink your blood will abide in you forever and enjoy eternal life. Keep me united to you through the Eucharist as a branch on the vine and nourish me so that I may produce fruit for your glory.

3. Ask one or more of the following questions:
   • In what way has this study challenged you the most?
   • How has this study deepened the experience of receiving communion for you?

4. Discuss lessons 25 through 30. Choose one or more of the questions for reflection and discussion from each lesson to discuss as a group.

5. Ask the group if they would like to study another book in the Threshold Bible Study series. Discuss the topic and dates, and make a decision among those interested. Ask the group members to suggest people they would like to invite to participate in the next study series.

6. Ask the group to discuss the insights that stand out most from this study over the past six weeks and how the Eucharist will hold a richer meaning from now on.

7. Conclude by praying aloud the following prayer or another of your own choosing:

Holy Spirit of God, you inspired the sacred writers of the Bible and you have guided our study during these weeks. Continue to deepen our love for the word of God in the holy Scriptures and draw us as disciples to the fullness of life you promise us through Christ's Eucharist. Sanctify us with the sacrificial love of Christ so that we may offer that love to those we meet. Bless us with the fire of your love.

Ordering Additional Studies

AVAILABLE TITLES IN THIS SERIES INCLUDE...

Advent Light • Angels of God • Eucharist
The Feasts of Judaism • The Holy Spirit and Spiritual Gifts
Jerusalem, the Holy City • The Lamb and the Beasts
Mysteries of the Rosary • The Names of Jesus
People of the Passion • Pilgrimage in the Footsteps of Jesus
The Resurrection and the Life • The Sacred Heart of Jesus
Stewardship of the Earth • The Tragic and Triumphant Cross

Jesus, the Messianic King (Part 1): Matthew 1–16
Jesus, the Messianic King (Part 2): Matthew 17–28
Jesus, the Word Made Flesh (Part 1): John 1–10
Jesus, the Word Made Flesh (Part 2): John 11–21
Jesus, the Suffering Servant (Part 1): Mark 1–8
Jesus, the Suffering Servant (Part 2): Mark 9–16
Jesus, the Compassionate Savior (Part 1): Luke 1–11
Jesus, the Compassionate Savior (Part 2): Luke 12–24
Church of the Holy Spirit (Part 1): Acts of the Apostles 1–14
Church of the Holy Spirit (Part 2): Acts of the Apostles 15–28

TWENTY THIRD 23rd PUBLICATIONS

To check availability or for a description
of each study, visit our website at
www.ThresholdBibleStudy.com
or call us at **1-800-321-0411**